DONUTS

DONUTS

OVER 50 INVENTIVE & EASY RECIPES
FOR ANY OCCASION

VICKY GRAHAM

Photography by **Joe Woodhouse**

hardie grant books

CONTENTS

INTRODUCTION

Hi! I'm Vicky. I set up Vicky's Donuts™ in 2015 after trips to see family in Toronto (where donuts are kind of a big deal!) inspired me to spread the love over here on the other side of the Atlantic. Sure, eating them is my fave thing to do, but the first time I tried making them, I just fell in love. From taking the time to mix the perfect dough, channelling your inner anger with a rolling pin, to plonking the little puffed-up rings into oil and watching them turn into pretty donuts within seconds; there's something very satisfying about the whole thing and it's my aim to get you hooked too.

I only properly got into baking a few years ago. I guess it started when I worked at a food magazine in my mid-twenties. My colleagues would show me their mood boards for photo shoots and lend me the tricks of the trade in food styling. I'd ask them a million questions about how to get into recipe writing and I'd follow them around the office like a puppy when the page proofs came back, so excited to see the end result of a long creative process.

At that time, I had the idea to do a similar thing with donuts. I really enjoyed making them at home, so I thought, 'Let's take some pics and stick them on Instagram!' And then I thought, 'Ooo! Wouldn't it be great if I could actually sell them, too?' So I decided to apply for a stall at a local market, asked my amazing mate, Kate Moross, (from award-winning Studio Moross) for help with branding and set up a little website. Friends of friends told their friends, who passed the word onto their friends, and suddenly I was getting business from strangers, which was the weirdest feeling ever. I soon began to realise that I have a love for feeding people. Even now, I get so much happiness from watching other people eat my food (yes, I realise that's kinda freaky but I've decided to roll with it).

I started from the tiny kitchen of a little rented flat in Dalston, East London, with my two very patient housemates as my in-house taste-testers. I'd get up at 5 a.m., before work, to fulfil orders, and then go and deliver them on my lunch break. Looking back on it, I must have been pretty tired all the time but the more I did it, the more I loved it, and I became determined to make it my full-time job. I was obsessed.

Today, we make anything up to 1,000 donuts in a day in the bakery, still in Dalston (just in a much bigger space!), and still in small batches,

'This book aims to pass on a little bit of that donut magic to your home kitchen.'

using the highest-quality ingredients. Luckily I don't have to be the baker, decorator, delivery guy and accountant all at once any more — thanks to my amazing team, we're now a little donut family.

This book aims to pass on a little bit of that donut magic to your home kitchen. Making donuts seems to have a rep for being a lengthy process that's super difficult to get right, but I'm here to prove to you that it's really not! I had zero expertise when I first started and I'm totally self-taught.

My goal is to give you a collection of hints, tips and recipes that I so wish was out when I first started. I tried and tried to find recipes to make my own and ended up geeking out on old American cookbooks, adapting them to make the ingredients a little nicer and make them easier to do from a home kitchen, so that you're not getting out of bed every four hours to feed your sourdough starter (yep, been there).

Hopefully, with some simple instructions, inventive flavours and fancy designs, I can turn you into a donut-making pro (and you'll have loads of fun in the process).

If you stick to these principles, you can't really go wrong:

1 Source good-quality ingredients. Why? They taste better!

2 Follow the recipe – baking is chemistry. Don't try to blag it or make changes until you've got it down.

3 Take your time and have fun! I'm at my happiest when sporting an apron, elbow-deep in dough, with a face full of flour. Get messy and embrace it.

I've included a selection of my favourite donuts that we make in the bakery every day, as well as a few new ones that I've tried to push the barriers with. There's also a selection of gluten-free and vegan recipes so that everybody can be in on the donut lovin'.

Anyhoo! Let's get to it. We've got some donuts to make.

HINTS & TIPS

A Brief History of Donuts

Traditionally, a donut is made from a yeasted enriched dough (one that contains milk, butter, eggs and/or sugar), which is then deep fried in oil. It's this method that makes them crispy on the outside and soft and squidgey on the inside – THE BEST! However, I understand that if you haven't fried a lot of foods before, you might want to ease yourself in by baking the donuts in the oven instead.

The main dough recipe that forms the basis of this book can either be baked or fried, and there's detailed instructions for both (page 21). Once you get the hang of the baked ones, please do give the fried ones a go – they're worth it, hands down, and so much fun to try, too.

One thing to note about making any of the recipes in this book is that these donuts are best eaten on the same day they're made, preferably within a few hours! There are no artificial preservatives in any of the doughs or batters (the best way to be) so they start to go stale around 12 hours after coming out of the oven or fryer. Of course, this just means that you HAVE to stuff your face after making them – ain't no excuses.

With any of the recipes that use yeast, it's important to note a few facts about the temperament of a yeasted dough:

1 When waiting for the dough to prove or rise (when the yeast releases little carbon-dioxide bubbles, allowing the dough to increase in size), it's going to be a much quicker process in a warm environment. We're super speedy at making donuts in the summer in the bakery because there's hardly any waiting around to do, whereas in the winter we have to allow a bit longer and rely on heaters or proving drawers (you can get these at home, too) to get things going.

2 A faster rise is not necessarily a tastier rise – the longer the rise, the better the depth of flavour this generally gives the dough.

3 Be gentle with dough! You might see some TV chefs slapping it about like it's tough, but it should be handled as little as possible to give you the best results.

◄ HINTS & TIPS

Essential Equipment

Donut tin (pan) for baked donuts and ring donut cutters for dough.

A large flat surface for rolling dough is essential.

Baking tray (pan): the donuts need a flat surface to lie on in order to prove properly and a baking tray is ideal for this.

Cutter: you can make donuts into pretty much any shape you fancy but the typical cutters we'll be using in this book are special donut cutters for dough rings. You can get them from most baking shops.

Deep-fat fryer (deep fryer): it's crazy how inexpensive good deep-fat fryers have become. However, if you don't want to be cluttering up your kitchen, a heavy-based saucepan will work just as well. Just make sure you use a digital thermometer, as you'll need to act as a human thermostat, adjusting the heat to get the temperature of the oil just right.

Donut tin (pan): essential if making cake donuts baked in the oven, but not essential for yeasted donuts. You can get these online or from baking shops.

Electric scales: although balance scales and mechanical scales look really pretty, they're not very accurate and can end up getting the quantities of your ingredients wrong, which, in baking, is a recipe for disaster (pun not intended). At home, I use digital flat scales that are accurate to 1 g (1/10 oz) and can weigh up to 5 kg (11 lb). These are a good investment that will see you through lots of baking.

Fish slice (turner): these are incredibly handy for manoeuvering donuts to the fryer. You want to make sure you handle the dough as carefully as possible so as not to lose any of the air inside and these guys are perfect at doing just that.

Large work surface: you'll need an even, flat surface that has enough space for you to roll out dough mega comfortably, without banging your head or your elbows on anything (spoken like a true Londoner who lives in a tiny flat!). Clearing the kitchen table of fruit bowls, or the kitchen worktop of toasters and kettles, works fine and dandy. Just make sure to give it a good old clean beforehand.

Mixing bowls: my fave mixing bowls are the plastic ones – they're durable and easy to scrape clean. When whipping up egg whites for fillings and toppings, be sure to use a metal or glass bowl – they don't hold on to fats as much, which can weigh down the super-light texture.

Piping bags: handy for filled donuts and intricate decoration with icing (frosting). It's best to get reusable ones as they're much more friendly to the environment, even if they are a bit awkward to clean. I don't really find the need to use nozzles. A nifty trick when cutting different size openings is to write on each bag exactly the size you've cut with a permanent marker.

Rolling pin: this can be plastic or wooden (or marble, if you're fancy), but the bigger the better – any extra force you can get to help roll out that dough comes in dead handy.

Non-Essential Equipment

Digital thermometer: I love mine! It offers assurance when frying donuts, making caramel or crème pâtissière. We use digital ones in the bakery that are accurate to the nearest 0.1°C (0.2°F). You can buy them for very little, so I think they're well worth it for peace of mind.

Dough scraper: these little tools are my fave thing ever. They can slice right through dough, which makes it super easy to portion, and are a dream at getting doughy residue and flour off your worktop when cleaning up.

Electric whisk (hand mixer): great for mixing up egg whites, buttercream, whipped cream, icings (frosting), glazes and crème pâtissière.

Food processor: handy for things like making nut butters and chopping chocolate. The batter for my recipe for the Pistachio & Orange Blossom donuts (page 77) is made entirely using a food processor.

Stand Mixer: these are great for kneading dough, so you don't have to wear your muscles out. Always make sure you set it on its lowest speed when making dough. I broke my first KitchenAid by kneading on a fast speed and wore out its motor (super sad face!). They are also mega handy for whipping up icings and fillings in a jiffy, if you don't have an electric whisk. They can be expensive to buy, but if you love baking, they're definitely worth the investment.

Ingredients

Butter: it always surprises me how much difference a good-quality butter can make to the taste and texture of a dough. Cheap butters are bland and watery whilst quality butters are rich and creamy – all of which you can taste in every bite. Always use unsalted butter unless otherwise specified.

Eggs: make sure they're free range! Not only is it good to be friendly to chickens but they're generally much better quality, too. Always use medium-sized eggs for accuracy.

Flour: the rule of thumb is, generally, the more you pay, the better the quality. My main donut dough, uses strong white bread flour (page 19), but some of my recipes use self-raising flour.

Food colouring: gels are much easier to use than liquids. They produce better results and are much less faff. Try to find natural ones if you can – most supermarkets now sell them.

Glazes and icings (frosting): what's the difference? A glaze is essentially a runnier version of icing. When making either, be sure to give it a good stir before dunking your donuts, as the surface can set super quickly and form a skin. If your icing or glaze is too thick, add a tiny bit of hot water to make it more malleable.

Milk: don't even talk to me about skimmed or semi-skimmed milk. It's not real milk. I use full-fat (whole) milk in my go-to batter, The Original (page 19), with a dairy-free alterntive for a vegan option (page 128).

Sugar: always use caster (superfine) sugar. It dissolves easily in doughs and batters, which helps them to rise without being weighed down. Some of the recipes call for using golden caster sugar. I prefer using granulated sugar to coat the outside of my donuts in, for added texture and crunch.

Vanilla bean paste: I use this all the time. You could also substitute vanilla extract. Just DON'T ever use essence – I don't even know what that stuff is.

Yeast: all of the dough recipes call for instant yeast. It's so easy to use and tastes great. If you want to use fresh yeast, just triple the amount and dissolve in some warm liquid with a little sugar for 10–15 minutes, until bubbles start to form on the surface.

RAISED DONUTS

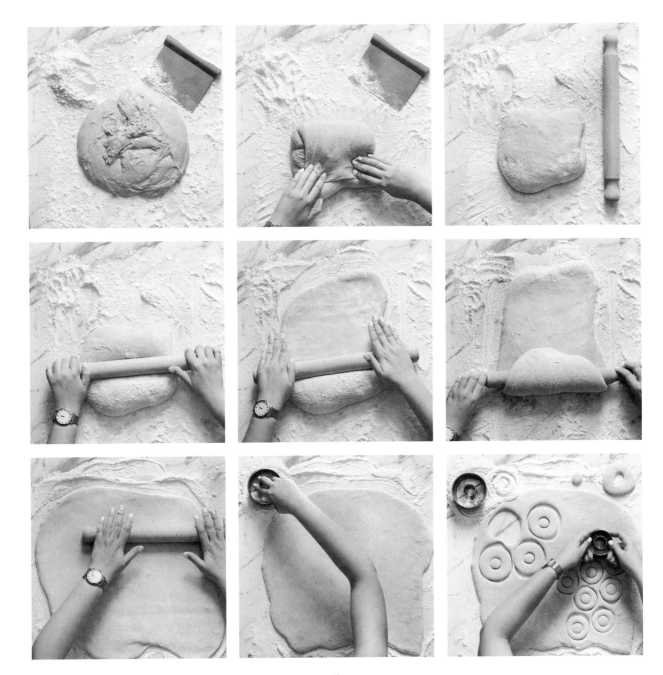

THE ORIGINAL

Our original raised donut recipe, made day in, day out at the bakery.

**Makes 12 regular donuts
or 24 minis**

750 g (1 lb 10 oz/5 cups) strong white
  bread flour, plus extra for dusting
80 g (3 oz/⅓ cup) caster (superfine) sugar
80 g (3 oz/⅔ stick) unsalted butter
15 g (½ oz/3 tsp) salt
21 g (¾ oz/6 tsp) instant dried yeast
  (3 packets)
3 medium eggs
240 ml (8 fl oz/1 cup) warm full-fat
  (whole) milk
140 ml (5 fl oz/½ cup) warm water
2 tbsp vegetable oil

---

stand mixer (optional)
rolling pin
dough scraper (optional)
cutters (in shape of your choice)

1   Place the flour, sugar and butter in a large bowl. Make 2 wells in the flour at opposite sides of the bowl and add the salt to one, and the yeast to the other.
2   Break in the eggs and then add the warm milk.
3   If using a stand mixer, attach the dough hook and mix on the slowest speed, whilst carefully pouring in the water, bit by bit. If you don't have a stand mixer, use one hand to bring the dough together and the other to pour in the water. Mix together until all the ingredients have been incorporated – you should end up with a sticky, wet mixture.
4   Continue kneading the dough on a slow setting for around 8 minutes or, by hand, on a floured surface for 10 minutes. When the dough has been kneaded enough, it'll be smooth, elastic and have a shiny surface.
5   Put the dough in a clean bowl and cover with a damp tea towel (dish towel) until doubled in size (anything between 20–90 minutes, depending on the temperature of your kitchen).
6   Grease 2 baking trays (baking pans) with 1 tablespoon of vegetable oil on each.
7   Cover your hands with flour and sprinkle a flat surface with more flour. Tip out the dough and knead with your hands to form a ball. Use a dough scraper, if you like, to help pick up all the doughy residue from the surface.
8   Sprinkle the rolling pin with flour and roll out the dough to around 2 cm (¾ in) thick.
9   Use a cutter to cut out your desired shapes and place onto the greased baking trays, spacing them out. Knead any leftover dough and roll out to repeat the process until you have used up all the dough. Leave to rise for around 10–20 minutes until the dough springs back when you touch it.
10   Cook the dough using one of the methods on page 21 and smother with your glaze or icing of choice!

FRYING & BAKING

Baked or fried? Frying your donuts will make them crispy and fluffy whilst baking them will make them soft and squidgy.

Frying Method

The original and most effective way of making donuts – this is how we do them in the bakery every day. Remember to be super careful when using hot oil. Keep any form of water away from the fryer or pan, move slowly to avoid any splashes and, if using a pan, always use a digital thermometer to make sure the oil doesn't get too hot.

3 litres (100 fl oz/12 cups) vegetable oil

1   Preheat a deep-fat fryer (deep fryer), or oil in a heavy-based pan, to 180°C (350°F).
2   Use a fish slice (turner) to carefully pick up each portion of dough and then carefully drop the dough into the fryer, cooking each one for around 60 seconds on each side, until golden brown in colour.
3   Remove with tongs and place on a baking tray (baking pan) lined with a paper towel to soak up any excess oil. Leave to cool.

Baking Method

These guys are sprayed with oil before and after they go into the oven to simulate the frying process. They have a lovely depth of flavour to them.

rapeseed oil spray

1   Preheat the oven to 220°C (430°F/Gas 7).
2   Fill a roasting dish with boiling water and place it at the bottom of the oven.
3   Spray the donuts with oil (around 3 spays per donut, as a general rule of thumb) and bake in the oven for 6 minutes.
4   Spray with oil again as soon as they leave the oven and leave to cool.

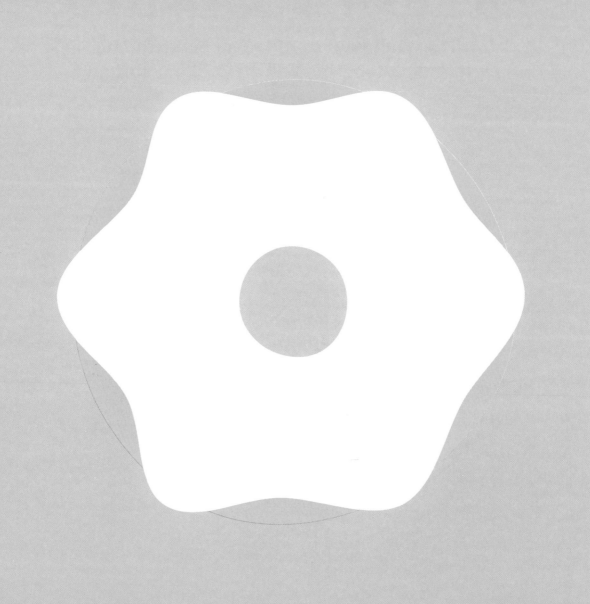

ICED
DONUTS

VANILLA BEAN

This icing is not only super tasty but versatile, too. You can add a little bit of natural food colouring to make it whatever colour you fancy.

**Covers 12 regular donuts
or 24 minis**

1 batch of The Original dough,
   fried or baked ⟶ P.19 & P.21

500 g (1 lb 2 oz/4 cups) icing
   (confectioner's) sugar
1 tsp vanilla bean paste
50 ml (2 fl oz/¼ cup) full-fat (whole) milk
30 g (1 oz/2 tbsp) sprinkles of your choice
   (made with natural colouring), to decorate

---

10 cm (4 in) ring cutter
   or 6 cm (2½ in) mini ring cutter

⟶ Wanna make it vegan? Turn to pages 128–129
to see how

1 Place the icing sugar, vanilla bean paste and half the milk into a bowl and stir.
2 Gradually add the rest of the milk, while mixing, until you end up with a smooth mixture.
3 Using a teaspoon, scoop up a blob of icing and twirl it around in a circular motion to stop any excess from dripping down.
4 Spoon the icing onto each donut and spread it out so that it evenly covers the top of the donut. If a little drips down the sides, don't worry, it adds to the effect! Add sprinkles and leave to set.

THE JAY DEE

Get your chocolate fix with this simple ganache, lightly sweetened with maple syrup and showered with sprinkles. The perfect emoji donut.

Covers 12 regular donuts or 24 minis

1 batch of The Original dough,
   fried or baked → P.19 & P.21

300 ml (10 fl oz/1¼ cups) double (heavy) cream
150 g (5 oz/1 cup) dark chocolate chips
   (at least 50% cocoa solids)
1 tbsp maple syrup
30 g (1 oz/2 tbsp) sprinkles (made with natural
   colouring), to decorate
---
10 cm (4 in) ring cutter
   or 6 cm (2½ in) mini ring cutter

1 Heat the cream in a small saucepan over a medium heat until bubbles start to form on the surface. Be super careful not to let it boil as this will prevent the glaze from being shiny later on (and ... we all about that shine!).

2 Put the chocolate chips in a medium-sized, heatproof bowl and pour over the hot cream. Using a spatula, give the mixture a good stir picking up any lumps of chocolate left behind on the sides and at the bottom.

3 Leave to cool for 2 minutes, add the maple syrup and give it another stir to combine.

4 Dip the donuts, top down, into the chocolatey mixture, covering them to around halfway down, then pull out and lay flat.

5 Leave the glaze to cool for around 10 minutes before scattering over the sprinkles from a height.

6 Allow to set a little before eating.

THE HOMER

Our most popular flavour! Named after the iconic donut in the TV show *The Simpsons*, this guy is an all time fave with our customers. Plus, no need for food colour here – all of the pinky goodness comes straight from the raspberry coulis.

**Covers 12 regular donuts
or 24 minis**

1 batch of The Original dough,
    fried or baked → P.19 & P.21

500 g (1 lb 2 oz/2 cups) icing
    (confectioner's) sugar
100 ml (3½ fl oz/scant ½ cup) Raspberry Coulis
→ P.146
zest and juice of 1 lemon
30 g (1 oz/2 tbsp) sprinkles (made with natural
    colouring)
- - -
10 cm (4 in) ring cutter
    or 6 cm (2½ in) mini ring cutter

1   Place the icing sugar, raspberry coulis, lemon zest and juice into a bowl and give it a good stir.
2   Using a teaspoon, scoop up a blob of icing and twirl it around in a circular motion to stop any excess from dripping down.
3   Spoon onto each donut and spread it so that it covers the whole surface.
4   Scatter the sprinkles over the iced donuts, from a height, covering the surface evenly.
5   Leave to set a little before eating.

THE GOLDEN GIRL

Whenever we bring these guys out at an event, they're one hundred per cent the first ones to go. There's something about that salt-and-sweet icing with the crunch of the pretzels.

Covers 12 regular donuts or 24 minis

1 batch of The Original dough, fried or baked → P.19 & P.21

60 g (2 oz/½ stick) unsalted butter
100 g (3½ oz/scant ½ cup) golden caster (superfine) sugar
20 g (¾ oz/⅛ cup) muscovado sugar
1 tbsp golden syrup (or dark corn syrup)
150 ml (5 fl oz/generous ½ cup) full-fat (whole) milk
½ tsp salt
300 g (10 ½ oz/2⅓ cups) icing (confectioner's) sugar
100 g (3½ oz/2 cups) pretzels, to decorate
100 g (3½ oz/⅔ cup) dark chocolate chips, to decorate

---

10 cm (4 in) ring cutter
or 6 cm (2½ in) mini ring cutter

1 Put the butter, sugars and syrup in a saucepan and place over a low heat, stirring continuously until the sugar has dissolved and the mixture starts to bubble.
2 Add the milk and keep stirring. If you notice any lumps of sugar, keep stirring over the heat until dissolved then add the salt.
3 Leave to cool to room temperature.
4 Place the icing sugar in a bowl and pour over three-quarters of the cooled caramel mixture. Give it a good mix until the icing sugar has dissolved. It will be very thick, but keep going!
5 Add the rest of the caramel mixture until you have a smooth, glossy icing.
6 Spoon the icing onto each donut and spread it so that it covers the whole surface.
7 Quickly top the donuts with the pretzels so that they stick to the surface. (If you are making the regular-sized donuts, 3 pretzels per donut is perfect.) Let them set whilst you make the chocolate sauce.
8 Melt the chocolate either in the microwave for around 1 minute, or in a glass bowl set over a pan with 5 cm (2 in) water, on a low heat.
9 Use a spoon to liberally drizzle the chocolate over the donuts. Enjoy!

BLOOD ORANGE

I get so excited when blood oranges come into season. The sweet and sour combo is mouthwateringly good.

**Covers 12 regular donuts
or 24 minis**

1 batch of The Original dough,
  fried or baked → P.19 & P.21

candied blood orange slices

1 blood orange

200 ml (7 fl oz/generous ¾ cup) water

200 g (7 oz/scant 1 cup) caster (superfine) sugar,
  plus 1 tbsp

blood orange icing (frosting)

2 blood oranges

500 g (1 lb 2 oz/4 cups) icing (confectioner's)
  sugar

hot water, to top up (if required)

---

10 cm (4 in) ring cutter
  or 6 cm (2½ in) mini ring cutter

1 To make the candied blood orange slices, cut the blood orange into very thin slices, around 5 mm (¼ in), and cut each of these in half. You'll need one slice per donut.

2 Put the water and the sugar into a large saucepan over a medium heat and bring it to the boil, stirring, until the sugar dissolves.

3 Turn down to a medium-low heat and place the orange slices in the pan.

4 Leave to simmer for 45 minutes until translucent, turning the slices every now and then to prevent them from sticking to the bottom of the pan.

5 Place the slices on a cooling rack and allow them to cool to room temperature.

6 Sprinkle the slices with the extra tablespoon of sugar to reduce the stickiness.

7 To make the icing, zest the blood oranges and squeeze to extract all the juice.

8 Place the icing sugar in a bowl and add the blood orange zest and the juice.

9 Mix together until you have a runny, but sturdy mixture, topping up with hot water if it needs loosening a little.

10 Carefully dunk each donut into the bowl until the icing covers it to around halfway.

11 Gently pull the donut back up – keeping the top down and slowly spinning the donut by 180 degrees or so – to let any excess drip back down into the bowl.

12 Place a candied orange slice on top of each donut and let it set a little before eating.

MATCHA

Traditionally used in Japanese tea ceremonies, matcha is not only well known for containing lots of nice antioxidants but also for its distinctive, yummy green tea flavour.

**Covers 12 regular donuts
or 24 minis**

1 batch of The Original dough,
    fried or baked ⟶ P.19 & P.21

500 g (1 lb 1 oz/2¼ cups) icing
    (confectioner's) sugar
1 tsp matcha powder
60 ml (2 fl oz/¼ cup) full-fat (whole) milk
- - -
10 cm (4 in) ring cutter
    or 6 cm (2½ in) mini ring cutter

1   Put the icing sugar and matcha powder into a bowl and gradually add the milk, stirring as you go.
2   Dip each donut all the way down into the mixture, covering the centre and the edges with the emerald glaze.
3   Lay the donuts on a wire rack, over a baking tray (baking pan), letting the excess glaze drip down before devouring.

HIBISCUS

Using hibiscus for this icing gives it a lovely fruity flavour and a pretty pink hue. Decorate with edible flowers for a full-on floral effect.

Covers 12 regular donuts or 24 minis

1 batch of The Original dough,
    fried or baked → P.19 & P.21

500 g (1 lb 1 oz/ 2¼ cups) icing
    (confectioner's) sugar
90 ml (3 fl oz/generous ⅓ cup) hibiscus syrup
a handful of mixed edible dried flowers,
    to decorate

---

10 cm (4 in) ring cutter
    or 6 cm (2½ in) mini ring cutter

→ You can buy hibiscus syrup online
or from specialist drinks shops
→ We source our edible flowers online
from maddocksfarmorganics.co.uk

1 Put the icing sugar in a bowl and gradually stir in the syrup. Mix well until combined.
2 Using a teaspoon, scoop up a blob of icing and twirl it around in a circular motion to stop any excess from dripping down.
3 Spoon the icing onto each donut and spread it out, so that it covers the whole surface.
4 Place edible flowers on top whilst the icing is still sticky. Allow the icing to set a little before eating.

◂ ICED DONUTS

COFFEE & WALNUT

A fresh take on one of my fave British cakes, this donut has the added bonus of a caffeine boost, perfect for that afternoon slump.

**Covers 12 regular donuts
or 24 minis**

1 batch of The Original dough,
  fried or baked → P.19 & P.21

30 g (1 oz/2 tbsp) caster (superfine) sugar
pinch of salt
100 g (3½ oz/scant 1 cup) walnuts, shelled and
  halved and rinsed in cold water
500g (1 lb 2 oz/4 cups) icing
  (confectioner's) sugar
40 ml (1½ fl oz/2½ tbsp) espresso
1 scant tbsp maple syrup
---
10 cm (4 in) ring cutter
  or 6 cm (2½ in) mini ring cutter

1   Preheat the oven to 180°C (350°F/Gas 4) and line a baking tray (baking pan) with baking paper (baking parchment).

2   Put the sugar and salt in a bowl. Place the walnuts into the bowl and give them a good toss in the sugar mixture, coating fully.

3   Lay the sugared walnuts on the baking tray, spreading them out evenly. Bake in the oven for 8–10 minutes until golden. Allow to cool.

4   Place the icing sugar in a bowl and gradually add the espresso and maple syrup to make a glossy icing.

5   Using a teaspoon, scoop up a blob of icing and twirl it around in a circular motion to stop any excess from dripping down.

6   Spoon onto each donut and spread it evenly, so that it covers the whole surface.

7   Scatter over the candied walnuts whilst the icing is sticky. Let the icing set a little before eating. I love this with a cup of hot coffee.

BOUNTY®

'What's that you say? A Bounty in donut form?' Yep, that's right! I went there.

**Covers 12 regular donuts
or 24 minis**

1 batch of The Original dough,
   fried or baked ⟶ P.19 & P.21

300 ml (10 fl oz/1¼ cups) double
   (heavy) cream
150 g (5 oz/1 cup) dark chocolate chips
   (at least 50% cocoa solids)
1 tsp coconut extract or 1 tbsp coconut rum
40 g (1½ oz/¾ cup) toasted coconut
   chips, to decorate
- - -
10 cm (4 in) ring cutter
   or 6 cm (2½ in) mini ring cutter

1   Heat the cream on a medium heat until bubbles start to form on the surface. Be super careful not to let it boil otherwise the chocolate glaze won't be shiny later.

2   Put the chocolate chips in a medium-sized heatproof bowl and pour over the hot cream.

3   Using a spatula, give the mixture a good stir, picking up any lumps of chocolate left behind on the sides and at the bottom.

4   Leave to cool for 2 minutes and then add the coconut extract or rum.

5   Dip the donuts, top down, into the chocolatey mixture, covering up to around halfway down, then pull out and lay flat.

6   Leave the glaze to cool for around 5 minutes before scattering over the coconut chips.

LAVENDER & HONEY
WITH EDIBLE FLOWERS

These are THE prettiest donuts to make. You can use as many or as few edible flowers as you fancy – but in terms of taste, less is more. It kind of starts to feel like you're eating a salad if you use too many!

**Covers 12 regular donuts
or 24 minis**

1 batch of The Original dough,
   fried or baked ⟶ P.19 & P.21

60 ml (2 fl oz/¼ cup) full-fat (whole) milk
½ tsp lavender flowers
500 g (1 lb 2 oz/4 cups) icing
   (confectioner's) sugar
1 tbsp good-quality honey
touch of lilac natural food colouring
a handful of fresh edible flowers
   (my faves are pansies, primulas
   and violas), to decorate.

- - -

10 cm (4 in) ring cutter
   or 6 cm (2½ in) mini ring cutter

⟶ We source our edible flowers online
from maddocksfarmorganics.co.uk

1   Put the milk and lavender flowers in a pan over a medium heat, stirring occasionally.
2   Just before it comes to the boil, lower the heat and simmer for 2 minutes.
3   Remove from the heat, strain through a sieve into a measuring cup.
4   Put the icing sugar in a bowl, add the honey and gradually stir in the lavender-infused milk. Add the food colouring.
5   Stir well until smooth and, using a teaspoon, scoop up a blob of icing and twirl it around in a circular motion to stop any excess from dripping down.
6   Spoon onto each donut and spread evenly over the surface.
7   Place the edible flowers on top and eat!

CARDAMOM & MILK

One of my favourite treats is a warm cardamom bun. I remember trying one a few years ago for the first time in Copenhagen, not even being a massive fan of cardamom, and becoming hooked on them. The combination of butter and sugar with the intense hit of cardamom pods is addictive! Of course, as soon as I returned to London I created my own donut recipe.

Covers 12 regular donuts or 24 minis

1 batch of The Original dough,
   fried or baked → P.19 & P.21

60 ml (2 fl oz/¼ cup) full-fat (whole) milk
2 tbsp crushed cardamom pods, seeds removed
½ tsp ground cinnamon
40 g (1½ oz/¼ stick) melted butter
500 g (1 lb 2 oz/4 cups) icing
   (confectioner's) sugar

---

10 cm (4 in) ring cutter
   or 6 cm (2½ in) mini ring cutter

1   Put the milk, 1 tablespoon of the cardamom pods and all of the cinnamon in a pan over a medium heat, stirring occasionally.
2   Just before it comes to the boil, lower the heat and simmer for 2 minutes.
3   Remove from the heat and leave to cool to room temperature.
4   Stir in the melted butter and add the icing sugar, one spoonful at a time. Mix until smooth.
5   Dip the donuts into the glaze, submerging each one to around three-quarters down.
6   While the glaze is still wet, sprinkle over the remaining cardamom.

FILLED DONUTS

Note:
All of the filled donuts are made by using a ring cutter to cut out the hole. However, instead of removing the dough from the centre, you leave it in for the dough's prove so that both the dough ring and the dough 'hole' rise together. Fry or bake the donut with the centre intact, but, once the donuts are cooked, carefully remove the inner hole using a sharp knife, leaving behind a thin layer of dough at the base to act as a barrier for the filling. Therefore, when you pick the donut up, the insides don't fall out. Simple!

THE REESE'S®

Named after the amazing peanut butter cups, these guys replicate that savoury peanut filling with the smooth hit of chocolate. The sugar coating and sprinkling of peanuts adds an extra depth that makes them one of our bestsellers.

Makes 12 regular donuts or 24 minis

1 batch of The Original dough, fried or baked → P.19 & P.21 centres left in place during proving and cooking → note on P.47

20 g (¾ oz/1½ tbsp) unsalted butter

450 g (1 lb/1⅔ cups) good-quality peanut butter (If you can, choose a peanut butter that doesn't contain palm oil)

¼ tsp salt

1 tsp vanilla bean paste

300 g (10½ oz/2⅓ cups) icing (confectioner's) sugar

300 ml (10 fl oz/1¼ cups) double (heavy) cream

300 g (10 oz/1⅓ cups) caster (superfine) sugar, to coat

200 g (7 oz/1¼ cups) dark chocolate chips (at least 50% cocoa solids)

peanuts, to decorate

---

10 cm (4 in) ring cutter or 6 cm (2½ in) mini ring cutter

piping bag

1 Using a sharp knife, carefully remove the centre of the donut, creating a hole, but making sure you leave a little dough at the bottom to hold in the filling. Set aside.

2 Beat the butter and peanut butter together until smooth.

3 Add the salt, vanilla bean paste and icing sugar and mix.

4 Gradually add the cream and combine thoroughly until smooth and creamy.

5 Put the mixture into a piping bag and cut the end to make a hole that measures around 2 cm (¾ in). Twist the top to stop the mixture escaping.

6 Place the donuts in a bowl with the sugar and toss to coat. You might need to do this one by one.

7 Get your piping bag and from the top down, constantly twisting the bag, gently squeeze the mixture out.

8 Fill each of the holes with the peanut cream, gently lifting up to create one big wodge. Make sure you keep the bag held in the same position – don't be tempted to move it around, or it will look messy.

9 Melt the chocolate either in the microwave for 1 minute, or in a heatproof glass bowl over a pan with 5 cm (2 in) water over a low heat.

10 Use a spoon to drizzle the chocolate generously over the donuts and then sprinkle over the peanuts. Serve straight away.

LEMON MERINGUE PIE

Lemon Curd: good. Meringue: good. Pie crust crumbs: goood! If you have a blowtorch, it's worth making the effort to give the meringue a good toasting.

**Makes 12 regular donuts
or 24 minis**

1 batch of The Original dough,
   fried or baked → P.19 & P.21
   centres left in place during
   proving and cooking → note on P.47

300 g (10½ oz/1⅓ cups) caster (superfine) sugar
1 batch of Lemon Curd → P.142
1 batch of Italian Meringue → P.143
60 g (2 oz/½ cup) shortcrust pastry crumbs
   (ready-made and good-quality), crushed

---

10 cm (4 in) ring cutter
   or 6 cm (2½ in) mini ring cutter
2 piping bags
blowtorch

1   Using a sharp knife, carefully remove the centre of each donut making sure you leave a little dough at the bottom to hold in the filling. Set aside.

2   Place the donuts in a bowl with the sugar and toss to coat. You might need to do this one by one.

3   Put the lemon curd into a piping bag and cut the tip to make a hole that measures around 2 cm (¾ in). Twist the top of the bag so that none of the curd escapes.

4   Fill the inside of the donut with the lemon curd, twisting the bag as you go.

5   Fill another piping bag with the Italian meringue, and make a cut at the tip of the bag around 1 cm (½ in). Twist the bag at the top to stop the mixture from escaping.

6   Starting from the centre of the donut, make a swirl with the meringue, turning the donut with your other hand as you go.

7   Carefully light a blowtorch to a medium heat and hold the flame over the meringue until it goes brown and toasty.

8   Sprinkle the pie crust crumbs over the top (not photographed) and devour.

APPLE PIE

I love making these in autumn, just as the leaves start to fall and the nights get longer; they're the perfect comfort food treat.

Makes 12 regular donuts

1 batch of The Original dough,
   fried or baked → P.19 & P.21
   centres left in place during
   proving and cooking → note on P.47

apple filling

1 kg (2 lb 3 oz) Bramley apples, peeled, cored
   and sliced into chunks
125 g (4 oz/generous ½ cup) golden caster
   (superfine) sugar
2 tsp ground cinnamon
½ tsp ground nutmeg
juice of 2 lemons

pie crumbs

100 g (3½ oz/⅔ cup) plain (all-purpose) flour
60 g (2 oz/¼ cup) caster (superfine) sugar
pinch of salt
60 g (2 oz/½ stick) chilled unsalted butter,
   cut into chunks

vanilla bean glaze

500 g (1 lb 2 oz/4 cups) icing
   (confectioner's) sugar
1 tsp vanilla bean paste
80 ml (2½ fl oz/⅓ cup) full-fat (whole) milk
---
10 cm (4 in) ring cutter

1   Using a sharp knife, carefully remove the centre of each donut, making sure you leave a little dough at the bottom to hold in the filling. Set aside.

2   To make the filling, put the apples, sugar, cinnamon, nutmeg and lemon juice in a heavy-based saucepan and cook over a medium heat for around 20 minutes, stirring occasionally, until the apples are soft but still hold their shape. Leave to cool.

3   Preheat the oven to 190°C (375°F/Gas 5) and line a baking tray (baking pan) with baking paper (baking parchment).

4   Now make the pie crumbs. Put the flour, sugar and salt into a bowl and add the butter, rubbing the ingredients into each other with your fingertips to make a crumb-like texture.

5   Spread the crumbs across the prepared tray and bake for 15 minutes until golden.

6   To make the glaze, combine the icing sugar, vanilla bean paste and milk in a bowl.

7   Dip the donuts into the glaze to cover the whole surface area and leave to set over a wire rack.

8   Fill each donut with around 1 tablespoon of the apple filling and finish with a sprinkling of the pie crumbs.

▲ FILLED DONUTS

BLUEBERRY CHEESECAKE

Tangy cheesecake filling, marbled with fruity blueberry compote: best kinda cheesecake ever.

Makes 12 regular donuts

1 batch of The Original dough,
   fried or baked ⟶ P.19 & P.21
   centres left in place during
   proving and cooking ⟶ note on P.47

200 g (7 oz/generous ⅔ cup) cream cheese
4 tbsp icing (confectioner's) sugar
zest and juice of 1 lemon
4 tbsp double (heavy) cream
1 batch of Blueberry Compote ⟶ P.144
300 g (10½ oz/1⅓ cups) caster (superfine) sugar
60 g (2 oz/½ cup) crushed digestive biscuits
   or Graham crackers, to decorate
blueberries, to decorate

---
10 cm (4 in) ring cutter
piping bag

1   Using a sharp knife, carefully remove the centre of each donut, making sure you leave a little dough at the bottom to hold in the filling. Set aside.

2   Beat together the cream cheese, icing sugar and lemon zest and juice.

3   Gradually add the cream and whisk until thick and smooth.

4   Carefully fold in the blueberry compote to make a super-pretty marbled effect. Transfer the mixture to a piping bag.

5   Place the donuts in a bowl with the sugar and toss to coat. You might need to do this one by one.

6   Make a cut at the tip of the bag of around 2 cm (¾ in). Twist the top of the bag to stop the filling escaping out of the top. Pipe in the blueberry cheesecake filling and finish with a sprinkling of crushed biscuits and a scattering of blueberries.

S'MORES

What is it about marshmallow, chocolate and biscuit (cookie)? So good! It may be the messiest donut you will ever eat. Extra points if you can eat one without licking your lips.

<u>Makes 12 regular donuts</u>
<u>or 24 minis</u>

1 batch of The Original dough,
   fried or baked → P.19 & P.21
   centres left in place during
   proving and cooking → note on P.47

300 ml (10 fl oz/1¼ cups) double
   (heavy) cream
150 g (5 oz/1 cup) dark chocolate chips
   (at least 50% cocoa solids)
1 jar of shop-bought marshmallow fluff
   (213 g/7½ oz)
60 g (2 oz/½ cup) crushed digestive biscuits
   or Graham crackers, to decorate
---
10 cm (4 in) ring cutter
   or 6 cm (2½ in) mini ring cutter

1 Using a sharp knife, carefully take out the centre of each donut, making sure you leave a little dough at the bottom to hold in the filling. Set aside.

2 Heat the cream over a medium heat until bubbles start to form on the surface. Be careful not to let it boil.

3 Put the chocolate chips in a medium-sized heatproof bowl and pour over the hot cream.

4 Using a spatula, give the mixture a good stir, picking up any lumps of chocolate left behind on the sides and at the bottom. Leave to cool a little.

5 Dip the donuts, top down, into the chocolatey mixture, covering up to around halfway down. Pull out of the chocolate and lay flat.

6 Spoon 1–2 teaspoons of the marshmallow fluff into each donut (depending which size you go for).

7 Sprinkle the digestive biscuits over the top and eat!

▲ FILLED DONUTS

RHUBARB & CUSTARD

I've never been a huge fan of plain old custard donuts, but bring rhubarb into the equation and now we're talking!

▲ FILLED DONUTS

Makes 12 regular donuts or 24 minis

1 batch of The Original dough,
  fried or baked → P.19 & P.21
  centres left in place during
  proving and cooking → note on P.47

1 kg (2 lb 3 oz) rhubarb
370 g (13 oz/1 ⅔ cups) caster (superfine) sugar
zest and juice of 1 orange
1 batch of Crème Pâtissière → P.140
pink edible glitter spray (optional), to decorate

---

10 cm (4 in) ring cutter
  or 6 cm (2½ in) mini ring cutter
piping bag

1   Preheat the oven to 150°C (300°F/Gas 2).
2   Using a sharp knife, carefully remove the centre of each donut, making sure you leave a little dough at the bottom to hold in the filling. Set aside.
3   Wash and chop the rhubarb into chunks measuring around 5 cm (2 in) and put onto a roasting tray. Sprinkle over 75 g (2½ oz/1⅓ cup) of the sugar, add in the orange zest and juice and stir.
4   Place in the oven and cook between 45 minutes to 1 hour until the rhubarb is tender. Leave to cool.
5   Place the donuts in a bowl with the remaining sugar and toss to coat. You might need to do this one by one.

6   Transfer the crème pâtissière to a piping bag and cut an opening about 2 cm (¾ in) at the tip. Twist the top of the bag to stop the custard escaping. Fill the centre of each donut with around 1 tablespoon of the crème pâtissière.
7   Top the donuts with the roasted rhubarb and drizzle over a little of the cooking syrup.
8   If using the edible glitter, evenly spray the tops of each rhubarb.

PIÑA COLADA

It's a fact* that if you sing the 'Piña Colada song' while making these, they're guaranteed to be tastier.

*Totally made up piece of information

Makes 12 regular donuts

1 batch of The Original dough,
   fried or baked ⟶ P.19 & P.21
   centres left in place during
   proving and cooking ⟶ note on P.47
1 batch of Pineapple Jam ⟶ P.145
morello cherries, to garnish
straws and cocktail stirrer, to decorate

coconut cream
250 g (9 oz) unsalted butter
500 g (1 lb 2 oz/4 cups) icing
   (confectioner's) sugar
60 ml (2 fl oz/¼ cup) coconut milk
30 ml (1 fl oz/2 tbsp) coconut rum (optional)

pineapple glaze
500 g (1 lb 2 oz/4 cups) icing
   (confectioner's) sugar
70 ml (2¼ fl oz/generous ¼ cup) pineapple juice

10 cm (4 in) ring cutter
piping bag

1 Using a sharp knife, carefully remove the centre of each donut, making sure you leave a little dough at the bottom to hold in the filling. Set aside.

2 To make coconut cream, beat the butter for 2 minutes until pale and smooth. Add the icing sugar, one spoonful at a time, whilst continuing to beat.

3 Gradually mix in the coconut milk and rum, if using. Transfer the mixture to a piping bag.

4 To make the glaze, mix the icing sugar with the pineapple juice until smooth and runny.

5 Dip the donuts into the glaze to cover the whole surface area and leave to set over a wire rack.

6 Fill the donuts with around 2 teaspoons of pineapple jam.

7 Cut an opening at the tip of the piping bag, measuring about 2 cm (¼ in). Twist the top of the bag to stop the cream escaping. Pipe a blob of coconut cream on top of the jam.

8 Finish each donut with a cherry, a straw and a cocktail stirrer.

▲ FILLED DONUTS

CHOCOLATE ORANGE

One of my fave flavour combinations ever. Using fresh orange zest really gives these guys a punch.

<u>**Makes 12 regular donuts or 24 minis**</u>

1 batch of The Original dough,
   fried or baked ⟶ P.19 & P.21
   centres left in place during
   proving and cooking ⟶ note on P.47

300 ml (10 fl oz/1¼ cups) double (heavy) cream
100 g (3½ fl oz/⅔ cup) dark chocolate chips
   (at least 50 per cent cocoa solids)
1 tbsp golden syrup (or dark corn syrup)
zest of 2 oranges
200 g (7 oz/scant 1 cup) caster (superfine) sugar
1 Terry's Chocolate Orange®,
   or 150 g (5 oz/1 cup) orange-flavoured
   chocolate decorations
gold edible glitter spray, to decorate

---

10 cm (4 in) ring cutter
   or 6 cm (2½ in) mini ring cutter piping bag
piping bag

1   Using a sharp knife, carefully remove the centre of each donut, making sure you leave a little dough at the bottom to hold in the filling. Set aside.
2   Heat the cream over a medium heat until bubbles start to form on the surface. Be careful not to let it boil.
3   Put the chocolate chips in a medium-sized heatproof bowl and pour over the hot cream.
4   Using a spatula, give the mixture a good stir, picking up any lumps of chocolate left on the sides and at the bottom.
5   Leave to cool for 2 minutes, add the golden syrup and give it another stir to combine.
6   Add the orange zest and stir again, before putting the mixture into a piping bag and chilling for around 2 hours.
7   Place the donuts in a bowl with the sugar and toss to coat. You might need to do this one by one.
8   Cut an opening at the tip of the piping bag measuring around 2 cm (¾ in). Fill the centre of each donut with a blob of the chilled chocolate-orange cream and top with a segment of chocolate orange.
9   Spray with gold edible glitter before serving.

BAKEWELL TART

If donuts had beauty pageants, this one would definitely be crowned the winner. The flaked almonds add a great crunch that combines super well with the raspberry coulis filling inside.

Makes 12 regular donuts or 24 minis

1 batch of The Original dough, fried or baked → P.19 & P.21 centres left in place during proving and cooking → note on P.47

500 g (1 lb 8 oz/2 cups) icing (confectioner's) sugar
1 tsp almond extract
60 ml (2 fl oz/¼ cup) full-fat (whole) milk
100 g (3½ oz/⅔ cup) flaked almonds
1 batch of Raspberry Coulis → P.146
red edible glitter, optional
12–24 fresh red cherries (depending on what size donut you make)
---
10 cm (4 in) ring cutter
or 6 cm (2½ in) mini ring cutter piping bag

1   Using a sharp knife, carefully take out the centre of each donut, making sure you leave a little dough at the bottom to hold in the filling. Set aside.

2   Make the almond icing by mixing the icing sugar, almond extract and milk together in a bowl until you have a smooth, semi-runny consistency.

3   Dunk each donut, top down into the icing, slowly pulling it out so that any excess drips down back into the bowl. Place on a wire rack.

4   Sprinkle the glazed donuts with the flaked almonds, letting them stick to the still gooey almond glaze.

5   Spoon 1–2 teaspoons of raspberry coulis (depending on which size you're making) inside each donut.

6   If using the edible glitter, place it a small bowl and run each cherry under a tap to make it damp. Dip the cherry into the edible glitter to cover it with sparkly goodness.

7   Place the sparkly cherries on top to finish.

CRÈME BRÛLÉE

Blasting these babies with a blowtorch gives them a crunchy caramel topping that when you bite, breaks into shards and oozes out the creamy custard filling. *C'est très bonne!*

**Makes 12 regular donuts
or 24 minis**

1 batch of The Original dough,
   fried or baked → P.19 & P.21
   centres left in place during
   proving and cooking → note on P.47

300 g (10½ oz/1⅓ cups) caster (superfine) sugar
1 batch of Crème Pâtissière → P.140
---
10 cm (4 in) ring cutter
   or 6 cm (2½ in) mini ring cutter piping bag
blowtorch

1 Using a sharp knife, carefully remove the centre of each donut, making sure you leave a little dough at the bottom to hold in the filling. Set aside.

2 Put 200 g (7 oz/scant 1 cup) of the sugar in a bowl. Place each donut into the bowl and toss to coat.

3 Spoon 1–2 teaspoons of the crème pâtissière into the donuts (depending on which size you're making) filling the centres of each one.

4 Sprinkle 1 teaspoon of the remaining sugar over each donut and blast with the blowtorch to crystallise the sugar. Be very careful not to overdo it — otherwise you might burn the sugar, which will make it taste bitter.

BANOFFEE PIE

By caramelising the bananas, you really bring out their flavours, making them a perfect combo with the custard.

**Makes 12 regular donuts
or 24 minis**

1 batch of The Original dough,
  fried or baked → P.19 & P.21
  centres left in place during
  proving and cooking → note on P.47

400 g (14 oz/1¾ cups) caster (superfine) sugar
2 bananas, peeled and diagonally sliced into
  strips measuring 5 mm (¼ in) thick
50 g (2 oz/½ stick) unsalted butter
1 batch of Crème Pâtissière → P.140

---

10 cm (4 in) ring cutter
  or 6 cm (2½ in) mini ring cutter piping bag

1 Using a sharp knife, carefully remove the centre of each donut, making sure you leave a little dough at the bottom to hold in the filling. Set aside.

2 Heat 100 g (3½ oz/scant ½ cup) of the sugar over a medium heat in a frying pan (skillet), until it caramelises.

3 Add the banana slices, shaking the pan to coat them in the caramel. Stir in the butter and heat for another 2 minutes.

4 Transfer the caramelised liquid plus some of the banana slices (you need to reserve at least 12–24 pieces for the garnish, depending on what size donut you make) to a bowl and stir in the crème pâtissière. Mix together until smooth and creamy.

5 Put the remaining sugar in a bowl with the donuts and toss to coat. You may need to do this one by one.

6 Spoon the banana custard into each of the holes and top with the reserved pieces of banana.

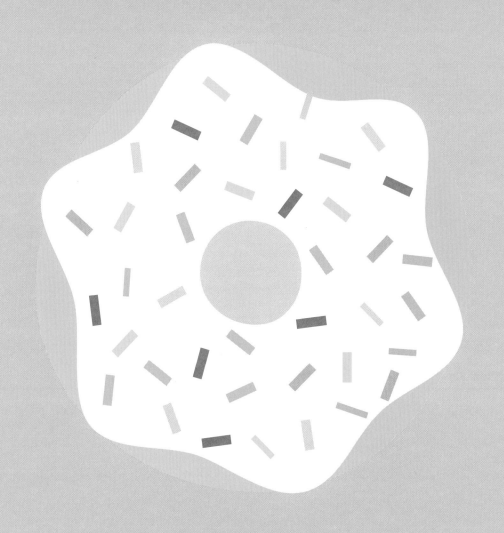

CAKE
DONUTS

CHOCOLATE & SALTED CARAMEL DONUTS

My second favourite dessert (after donuts obvs) is salted caramel brownies, so I thought I'd give it a go combining the two in a basic cake mixture recipe. Dream team.

Makes 12 regular donuts or 24 minis

160 g (6 oz/ scant 1½ sticks) unsalted butter (at room temperature), plus extra for greasing
200 g (7 oz/1 cup) caster (superfine) sugar
180 g (6⅓ oz/scant 1 cup) plain (all-purpose) flour
60 g (1¾ oz/¼ cup) cocoa powder
1 tsp baking powder
½ tsp bicarbonate of soda (baking soda)
½ tsp salt
1 tsp vanilla bean paste
150 ml (5 fl oz/½ cup) buttermilk
2 medium eggs (beaten)
1 batch of Salted Caramel → P.141

2 × 12-hole donut tin (pan)
   or 2 × 6-hole donut tin (pan

---

1 Heat oven to 180°C (350°F/ Gas 4) and liberally grease the donut tin with butter.

2 Beat the butter and sugar until pale and fluffy.

3 Add the flour, cocoa powder, baking powder, bicarbonate of soda and salt and mix.

4 Stir in the vanilla bean paste, buttermilk and eggs and beat again until combined.

5 Pour the mixture into the donut tin, filling each hole around two-thirds of the way up.

6 Bake in the oven for 10–12 minutes, until a skewer or cocktail stick inserted in the centre comes out clean. Leave to cool before transferring to a wire rack.

7 To make the salted caramel, melt the butter and sugars in a saucepan over a gentle heat, until the butter has melted and sugar has dissolved.

8 Add the cream and salt and continue to stir on the heat until you're left with a gloopy caramel mixture. Leave to cool.

9 Spread the caramel on top of each donut and sprinkle with sea salt.

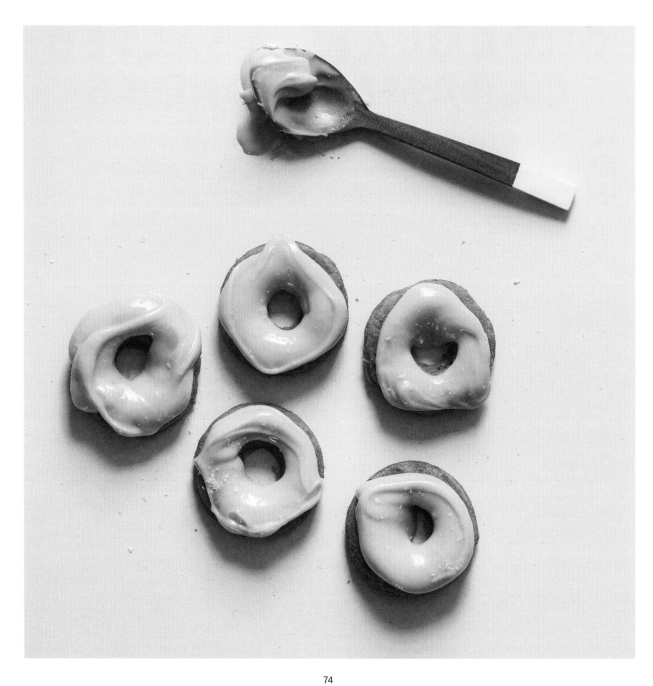

BANANA BREAD & MAPLE SYRUP

The more questionable the ripeness of the bananas, the better! You want them to be super overripe and gooey to make the cake mixture extra yum.

**Makes 12 regular donuts
or 24 minis**

140 g (5 oz/1 ¼ sticks) unsalted butter, plus extra for greasing
125 g (4 oz/generous ½ cup) caster (superfine) sugar
2 medium eggs
140 g (5 oz/scant 1 cup) plain (all-purpose) flour
2 tsp baking powder
2 ripe bananas, peeled and mashed
pinch of sea salt flakes

maple syrup icing (frosting)

300 g (10½ oz/2½ cups) icing (confectioner's) sugar
180 ml (6 fl oz/¾ cups) maple syrup

---

2 × 12-hole donut tin (pan)
    or 2 × 6-hole donut tin (pan

1 Preheat the oven to 180°C (350°F/Gas 4) and liberally grease the donut tin with butter.

2 Cream the butter and sugar until pale and fluffy and add the eggs, one at a time, adding 1 tablespoon of flour each time.

3 Fold in the remaining flour, baking powder and the mashed bananas.

4 Pour the mixture into the donut tin, filling each hole around two-thirds of the way up.

5 Bake in the oven for 12–14 minutes, until a skewer or cocktail stick inserted in the centre comes out clean. Leave to cool before transferring to a wire rack.

6 To make the icing, combine the icing sugar and maple syrup and mix until smooth.

7 Spoon the glaze onto the cooled donuts and return to the wire rack to set.

8 Sprinkle with sea salt flakes to finish.

PISTACHIO & ORANGE BLOSSOM

The pistachio in this cake mixture give these guys a rich flavour and unique texture, which perfectly couples with the orange blossom icing (frosting).

Makes 12 regular donuts or 24 minis

170 g (6 oz/1½ sticks) unsalted butter, plus extra for greasing
75 g (2½ oz/½ cup) pistachios, shelled, plus extra roughly chopped, to garnish
170 g (6 oz/1¾ cup) caster (superfine) sugar
165 g (6 oz/¾ cup) plain (all-purpose) flour
2 tsp baking powder
¼ tsp bicarbonate of soda (baking soda)
3 medium eggs
2 tbsp full-fate (whole) milk (if needed)

orange blossom icing (frosting)

500 g (1 lb 2 oz/4 cups) icing (confectioner's) sugar
1 tsp orange blossom water
zest and juice of 1 orange
---
2 × 12-hole donut tin (pan)
or 2 × 6-hole donut tin (pan

1 Heat the oven to 180°C (350°F/Gas 4) and liberally grease the donut tin (pan) with butter.

2 Put the whole pistachios into a food processor and blitz until fine.

3 Add the butter, sugar, flour, baking powder, bicarbonate of soda, eggs and continue to mix, until smooth.

4 Add the milk if it looks too thick — it should be the consistency of a thick custard.

5 Pour the mixture into the donut tin, filling each hole around two-thirds of the way up.

6 Bake in the oven for 12–14 minutes, until a skewer or cocktail stick inserted in the centre comes out clean. Leave to cool before putting onto a wire rack.

7 To make the icing, mix the icing sugar with the orange blossom water, orange zest and juice.

8 Using a spoon, spread the orange icing and spoon on top of each donut, letting any excess drip down the edges.

9 Sprinkle over the reserved chopped pistachios.

BIRTHDAY CAKE

Whenever I make these, I feel like a kid at a birthday party! Make sure to find the chunkiest sprinkles you can get your hands on so they hold their shape in the mixture to give you that 'funfetti' effect.

**Makes 12 regular donuts
or 24 minis**

180 g (6½ oz/1¾ sticks) unsalted butter,
   plus extra for greasing tin
180 g (6½ oz/¾ cup) caster (superfine) sugar
3 medium eggs
180 g (6½ oz/1¾ cups) sifted self-raising flour
1 tsp vanilla bean paste
1 tsp baking powder
70 g (2½ oz/⅓ cup, plus 1 tbsp) sprinkles
   (big, chunky and colourful ones are best),
   plus extra for decoration
pinch of salt
2 tbsp full-fat (whole) milk (if needed)

vanilla bean icing (frosting)

300 g (10½ oz/2½ cups) icing
   (confectioner's) sugar
½ tsp vanilla bean paste
30 ml (1 fl oz/2 tbsp) whole milk
---
2 × 12-hole donut tin (pan)
   or 2 × 6-hole donut tin (pan)

1   Heat the oven to 180°C (350°F/Gas 4) and liberally grease the donut tin with butter.

2   Put the butter and sugar in a mixing bowl and whisk until pale and fluffy.

3   Beat in the eggs, one at a time, adding a spoonful of flour each time.

4   Gently fold in the rest of the flour with the vanilla bean paste, baking powder, sprinkles and salt. Add the milk if it seems stiff.

5   Pour the mixture into the donut tin, filling each hole around two-thirds of the way up.

6   Bake in the oven for 12–14 minutes until a skewer or cocktail stick inserted in the centre comes out clean. Leave to cool before transferring to a wire rack.

7   To make the icing, place the icing sugar, vanilla bean paste and half of the milk into a bowl and stir.

8   Gradually add the rest of the milk, stirring, until you end up with a smooth mixture.

9   Carefully dunk each of the cooled cake donuts into the bowl until the icing covers it around halfway. Gently pull the donut back up, keeping the top down and slowly spinning it around by 180 degrees or so, to let any excess drip back down into the bowl.

10   Decorate with the giant sprinkles.

GINGER & CREAM CHEESE

My mum makes the bestest ginger cake and I've adapted this from her recipe, which teams perfectly with cream cheese frosting.

Makes 12 regular donuts or 24 minis

100 g (3½ oz/⅘ stick) unsalted butter, plus extra for greasing
250 g (9 oz/1⅔ cups) self-raising flour
4 tsp dried ginger
1 tsp baking powder
½ tsp salt
170 ml (6 fl oz/⅔ cup) hot water
100 g (3½ oz/½ cup) demerara sugar
150 g (5 oz/generous ⅓ cup) golden syrup (dark corn syrup)
1 medium egg

cream cheese icing (frosting)

80 g (3 oz/⅔ stick) unsalted butter
120 g (4 oz/½ cup) cream cheese
400 g (14 oz/3¼ cups) icing (confectioner's) sugar
crushed ginger biscuits (cookies), to decorate

- - -

2 × 12-hole donut tin (pan)
 or 2 × 6-hole donut tin (pan

1   Heat the oven to 180°C (350°F/Gas 4) and liberally grease the donut tin (pan) with butter.
2   Mix the flour, ginger, baking powder and salt in a bowl.
3   Whisk together the hot water, butter, sugar and syrup.
4   Add the egg to the dry mixture, followed by the wet mixture and beat together.
5   Pour the mixture into the donut tin, filling each hole around two-thirds of the way up. Bake for 15–18 minutes, until a skewer or cocktail stick inserted into the centre comes out clean. Leave to cool fully before transferring to a wire rack.
6   To make the icing, beat the butter and cream cheese until pale and smooth.
7   Add the icing sugar to a large bowl and stir in the cream-cheese mixture, two spoonfuls at a time, until smooth and creamy.
8   Using a teaspoon, scoop up a blob of icing onto each donut and spread it so that it covers the whole surface.
9   Sprinkle over the crushed ginger biscuits.

DESIGN

SKILLZ

PARTY RING DONUTS

Party ring biscuits were a staple of every party worth going to as a kid! They're even cuter in donut form and super fun to make.

Makes 24 mini donuts

1 batch of The Original dough,
  fried or baked → P.19 & P.21

1 batch of Vanilla Bean icing → P.25
pink, lilac and yellow natural food colouring
---
6 cm (2½ in) ring cutter
3 piping bags
cocktail sticks

1   Divide the vanilla bean icing among 3 bowls and colour one with pink, one with lilac and one with yellow food colouring.

2   Fill 3 piping bags with around one-third of the coloured-icing and cut a hole in the tip of each piping bag, measuring around 5 mm (¼ in). Twist the top of each bag to stop the icing escaping.

3   Dip a mini donut, top down, into one of the bowls of icing to around halfway, and gently pull back up.

4   In a contrasting colour, immediately ice 3 lines across the donut — be quick, we don't want the icing to dry yet!

5   Using a cocktail stick, drag 3 lines at a 90-degree angle to the ones you've just made, to create a feathering effect. Repeat for the remaining donuts.

6   Allow the icing to set before eating.

PIZZA DONUTS

'You wanna pizza me?' The perfect food for a sleepover – put your jammies on, stick on Ferris Bueller and dive in.

Makes 24 triangles

1 batch of The Original dough → P.19

1 portion Vanilla Bean icing → P.25
yellow and red natural food colouring
200g (7 oz) fondant icing
   (shop-bought is fine, no judgement!)
---
8 cm (3¼ in) triangle cutter
2 cm (¾ in) tiny circle cutter

1 Using a triangle cutter, cut out 24 triangle shapes. Bake or fry, following the instructions on page 21 and leave to cool.

2 Whilst waiting for them to cool, add a drop of yellow food colouring to the vanilla bean icing.

3 Add a drop of red food colouring to the fondant icing and mix in well. Roll the fondant out to around 3 mm (⅛ in) thick. Cut out tiny little circles with the round cutter — these will be your 'pepperoni'.

4 Give the yellow vanilla icing a good stir and dip each triangle, face down, into the bowl, covering the surface. Place the 'pepperoni' on top while the icing is still wet and sticky. Allow to set a little before eating.

PINEAPPLE DONUTS

Totally tropical and super fun to make! The green stems are made with coloured white chocolate. Cool, huh?

Makes 12 regular donuts

1 batch of The Original dough,
   fried or baked ⟶ P.19 & P.21

200 g (7 oz/1⅓ cups) white chocolate chips
drop of oil-based green natural food colouring
   (suitable for use in chocolate)
1 batch of Vanilla Bean icing ⟶ P.25
yellow and brown natural food colouring
---
10 cm (4 in) ring cutter
2 piping bags
cocktail stick

1   Melt the white chocolate either in the microwave for around 1 minute or in a heatproof glass bowl over a pan containing 5 cm (2 in) water, on a low heat. If you want to get really technical, use a probe thermometer to check the temperature – it should be at 28–29°C (82–84°F).

2   Add the green food colouring to the chocolate and mix well.

3   Place the green chocolate in a piping bag and cut an opening measuring about 5 mm (¼ in) in the tip of the bag. Twist the top of the bag to stop the chocolate escaping.

4   Line a baking tray (baking pan) with baking paper (baking parchment) and test a little of the chocolate. You want the chocolate to stay in place as it leaves the piping bag; if it's too runny, leave it to cool for a couple of minutes before testing again.

Continues ⟶

5 Make lines with the chocolate in the shape of a tuft. Add 2 cm (¾ in) vertical lines underneath – almost like you're making a cocktail stirrer – with the pineapple tuft sitting at the top. Leave to set (see photo for guide).

6 Divide the vanilla icing among two bowls.

7 Add a smudge of the yellow food colouring to one of the bowls and a smudge of brown to the other. Mix both well.

8 Carefully dunk each donut into the yellow vanilla icing until it covers it around halfway.

9 Gently pull the donut back up, keeping the top down and slowly spinning the donut around by 180 degrees or so, to let any excess drip back down into the bowl. Leave to set.

10 Put the brown icing into a piping bag and cut a hole around 5 mm (¼ in) in the tip. Twist the top of the bag to stop the icing escaping.

11 Using a cocktail stick, make a hole at the top of each donut and insert the green chocolate tuft so that it protrudes.

12 Using the brown icing, pipe diagonal lines in opposite directions, like a lattice, across the donut and finish off with dots in the centre.

MARBLED DONUTS

Marbles are HUGE right now! Have a go at these and try experimenting with different colours.

Makes 24 minis

1 batch of The Original dough,
   fried or baked → P.19 & P.21

1 batch of Vanilla Bean icing → P.25
natural food colouring in your choice of colours

---

6 cm (2½ in) ring cutter
cocktail stick

1   Depending on how many colours you'd like to make, divide the icing into as many bowls as you need and add a drop of food colouring to each one. Give each bowl a good stir.

2   Take a separate, empty bowl and spoon a little of each of the colours into it.

3   Using a cocktail stick, drag the colours into each other to create a marbled effect. If you find that the colours have begun to mix a little too much, repeat the process of spooning each of the colours into a bowl and mixing together with the cocktail stick again.

4   Carefully dunk each donut into the marbled icing until it covers it around halfway.

5   Gently pull the donut back up, keeping the top down and slowly spinning the donut around by 180 degrees or so, to let any excess drip back down into the bowl. Leave the icing to set before eating.

▲ DESIGN SKILLZ

GALAXY DONUTS

I first made these for a film premiere of the movie *Passengers* (soft brag) and they've become one of our most requested designs since. Watching the icing as it smooths over the donut is mesmerising!

Makes 12 regular donuts

1 batch of The Original dough,
    fried or baked → P.19 & 21

1 batch of Vanilla Bean icing → P.25
dark blue and dark pink natural food colouring
silver edible glitter
---
6 cm (4 in) ring cutter
cocktail sticks

1 Divide the vanilla bean icing into 3 bowls. Colour one bowl with dark blue food colour, one with dark pink and leave the last bowl white. Take a separate empty bowl and spoon a little of each icing into it. Using a cocktail stick, drag the colours into each other to create a marble effect.

2 Carefully dunk each donut into the marbled icing until it covers it around halfway.

3 Gently pull the donut back up, keeping the top down and slowly spinning the donut by around 180 degrees or so, to let any excess drip back down into the bowl. Leave to set.

4 Once the icing has set, sprinkle with the silver edible glitter to make your donuts look outta this world!

DONUT FRIES

A little bit of fun – these are a good snack for a night in when you want to sacriFRIES savoury and go for something sweet. Just like churros, these guys should be eaten fresh from the fryer, while still warm, for maximum yum-ness.

Makes 24 fries (4 regular portions/2 supersize portions)

1 batch of The Original dough → P.19
150 g (5 oz/¾ cup) caster (superfine) sugar

raspberry 'ketchup'
100g (3½ oz/scant 1 cup) raspberries
2 tsp icing (confectioner's) sugar
juice of ½ lemon

white chocolate 'mayonnaise'
50ml (2 fl oz/2¼ cup) double (heavy) cream
100g (3½ oz) white chocolate, broken into pieces

1 Make the dough following the recipe on page 19, up to step 8. Roll out the dough to around 2 cm (¾ in) thick and into a square shape (or as near as you can get to one).
2 Using a sharp knife, cut out strips of dough measuring around 1½ cm (½ in) in thickness.
3 Repeat the process until you end up with around 6–10 strips of dough.
4 Cut your strips into smaller pieces (between 4–8 cm/1½-3 in) so that they resemble fries. It's good if they look different to each other — that's how real fries are meant to be!
5 Using the frying method on page 21, fry the strips at 180°C (350°F) until golden brown, using either a metal spoon or metal tongs to move them around in the oil to make sure they're cooked from all sides.
6 Once cooked, drain them on a baking tray (baking pan) lined with paper towels until they're cool enough to touch.
7 Put the sugar into a medium-sized bowl and tip in the donut strips, three at a time, coating them with sugar.

8 To make the raspberry 'ketchup', put the raspberries, icing sugar and lemon juice into a pan and place on a low heat until the raspberries break down.
9 Take off the heat and either transfer to a food process and blitz until smooth or blend with a hand-blender.
10 Once smooth, pass through a sieve to remove any pips and place into a small dish, ready for some dunking.
11 Finally, get your white chocolate 'mayonnaise' ready by heating the double cream in a saucepan on a low heat until it simmers – be careful not to boil it.
12 Add the white chocolate pieces and stir. Leave for a couple of minutes to let the chocolate fully melt and stir again until all combined. Transfer to a small dish.
13 You can either go all out and place the strips into some fries containers or if you wanna keep it simple, place them into a bowl. Dip the fries into the sauces and scoff immediately.

▲ DESIGN SKILLZ

CELE
BRATE!

MINT CHOC CHIP CHRISTMAS DONUTS

It ain't Christmas without some mint chocolate! The popping candy gives every mouthful of these a little snap.

Makes 12 regular donuts or 24 minis

1 batch of The Original dough,
   fried or baked → P.19 & 21
40 g (1½ oz/2½ tbsp) chocolate-coated popping
   candy, to decorate

dark chocolate ganache
300 ml (10 fl oz/1¼ cups) double (heavy) cream
150 g (5 oz/1 cup) dark chocolate chips
   (at least 50% cocoa solids)

peppermint icing (frosting)
200 g (7 oz/1⅔ cups) icing
   (confectioner's) sugar
1 tsp peppermint extract
2 tsp full-fat (whole) milk
green natural food colouring

---

10 cm (4 in) ring cutter
piping bag

1   For the ganache, heat the cream on a medium heat until bubbles start to form on the surface. Be super careful not to let it boil as this will prevent the glaze from being shiny later on.
2   Put the chocolate chips in a medium-sized heatproof bowl and pour over the hot cream.
3   Using a spatula, give the mixture a good stir, picking up any lumps of chocolate left behind on the sides and at the bottom.
4   Leave for 2 minutes and then give it another stir until all the chocolate has melted into a glossy colour.
5   Dip the donuts, top down, into the chocolatey mixture, covering them to around halfway down. Immediately pull out and lay flat.
6   For the peppermint icing, mix together the icing sugar, peppermint extract and milk into a thickish icing. Add the green food colouring and put into a piping bag. Cut an opening measuring about 7 mm (⅓ in) in the tip of the bag. Twist the top of the bag to stop the icing escaping.

7   Once the chocolate ganache has set on the donuts (it should look really dark brown and will stay in place when prodded), pipe the mint icing in a swirly motion over the donuts.
8   Sprinkle with the popping candy and enjoy!

CELEBRATE!

MINCE PIE CHRISTMAS DONUTS

Not much to say about this one really! Mince pie, in a donut. All your Christmas dreams come true.

Makes 12 regular donuts

1 batch of The Original dough,
   fried or baked → P.19 & 21
   centres left in place during
   proving and cooking → note on P.47
12 tbsp good-quality mincemeat
   (not the meaty, Rachel-from-*Friends* kind, but
   the sweet stuff!)
edible gold glitter, to decorate

pie crumbs

100 g (3½ oz/⅔ cup) plain (all-purpose) flour
60 g (2 oz/1/4 cup) caster (superfine) sugar
pinch of salt
60 g (2 oz/½ stick) chilled unsalted butter,
   cut into chunks

cinnamon glaze

300 g (10½ oz/2½ cups) icing
   (confectioner's) sugar
2 tsp ground cinnamon
60 ml (2 fl oz/¼ cup) full-fat (whole) milk
---
10 cm (4 in) ring cutter

1 Preheat the oven to 190°C (375°F/ Gas 5) and line a baking tray (baking pan) with baking paper (baking parchment).
2 Using a sharp knife, carefully remove the centre of each donut, making sure you leave a little dough at the bottom to hold in the filling.
3 Prepare the pie crumbs by mixing together the flour, sugar and salt into a bowl. Add the butter, rubbing the ingredients with your fingertips to make a crumb-like texture.
4 Spread the crumbs across the baking tray and bake for 15 minutes until golden.
5 Heat the mincemeat in a pan over a medium heat until the suet melts. Leave to one side.
6 To make the glaze, combine the icing sugar, cinnamon and milk together.
7 Dip the donuts into the glaze to cover the whole surface area and leave to set over a wire rack.

8 Fill the donuts with around 1 tablespoon of the mincemeat and finish with a sprinkling of the pie crumbs.
9 Sprinkle with edible glitter and serve while still warm.

▲ CELEBRATE!

FRIED EGG EASTER DONUTS

'How do you like your eggs in the morning?' Ummmm, made from dough and covered in icing, please!

Makes 12 regular donuts

1 batch of The Original dough → P.19
plus donut holes from the insides of each ring
1 batch of Vanilla Bean icing → P.25
orange natural food colouring

---

10 cm (4 in) ring cutter

1   Make the dough recipe as on page 19 to produce 12 rings, taking out the holes from each donut ring and frying separately to give you donut holes (page 21).

2   Divide the vanilla icing into 2 bowls to a ratio of 1:4.

3   Place a small amount of orange food colouring into the smaller batch of icing and mix well.

4   Dip each of the donut holes into the orange icing and leave to set – these will be the yolks.

5   Give the remaining white icing a good stir and dip in the rings, one by one – these will be your egg whites.

6   Place each of the orange donut holes into the centre to form your fried egg and let the icing set before serving.

PUMPKIN SPICED HALLOWEEN DONUTS

Any excuse to add pumpkin spice to a recipe and I'm there! You can get pumpkin cutters from kitchen shops or online.

Makes 12 regular donuts

1 batch of The Original dough → P.19

spiced pumpkin filling

110 g (3¾ oz/1 stick) unsalted butter
300 g (10½ oz/2⅓ cups) icing (confectioner's) sugar
40 g (1½ oz/2½ tbsp) pumpkin purée
2 tsp ground cinnamon
½ tsp ground nutmeg
1 tsp vanilla bean paste
3 tbsp double (heavy) cream

cinnamon icing (frosting)

700 g (1 lb 9 oz/5⅔ cups) icing (confectioner's) sugar
2 tsp ground cinnamon
75 ml (2½ fl oz/⅓ cup) full-fat (whole) milk
black and orange natural food colouring

---

pumpkin-shaped cutter

1 Using a special pumpkin-shaped cutter, cut out the dough. Bake or fry the donuts, following the instructions on page 21. Leave to cool on a wire rack.

2 Once cooled, poke a hole into the base of the pumpkin shapes with a small, sharp knife – this is where we're going to pipe the pumpkin cream filling later.

3 Make the pumpkin filling. Using either a stand mixer or electric whisk, whisk the butter until pale and fluffy (around 2 minutes) and add two-thirds of the icing sugar, one spoonful at time, mixing in-between each addition.

4 Add the pumpkin purée, cinnamon, nutmeg and vanilla bean paste with the rest of the icing sugar and beat again. Add the double cream and beat until smooth.

5 Transfer the mixture to a piping bag and cut an opening measuring 1 cm (½ in). Twist the top of the bag to stop the filling from escaping.

6 Insert the end of the piping bag into the donut holes and squeeze gently until the the donut begins to puff up.

7 Make the cinnamon icing by placing the icing sugar, cinnamon and half of the milk into a bowl. Stir together then gradually add the rest of the milk, stirring continually, until you end up with a smooth mixture.

8 Put 2 tablespoons of the cinnamon icing into a separate bowl, mix in the black food colouring and place in a piping bag, cutting a hole measuring around 5 mm (¼ in) in the tip. Twist the top of the bag to stop the icing escaping.

9 Mix the rest of the icing with the orange food colouring and carefully dunk each donut into the bowl, covering the surface evenly.

10 Gently pull the donut back up, keeping the top down and slowly spinning the donut around by 180 degrees or so, to let any excess drip back down into the bowl. Leave to set.

11 Fill a second piping bag with the black icing, cutting the tip and twisting the top of the bag, as before. Carefully pipe on the Jack O'Lantern's details then serve!

▲ CELEBRATE!

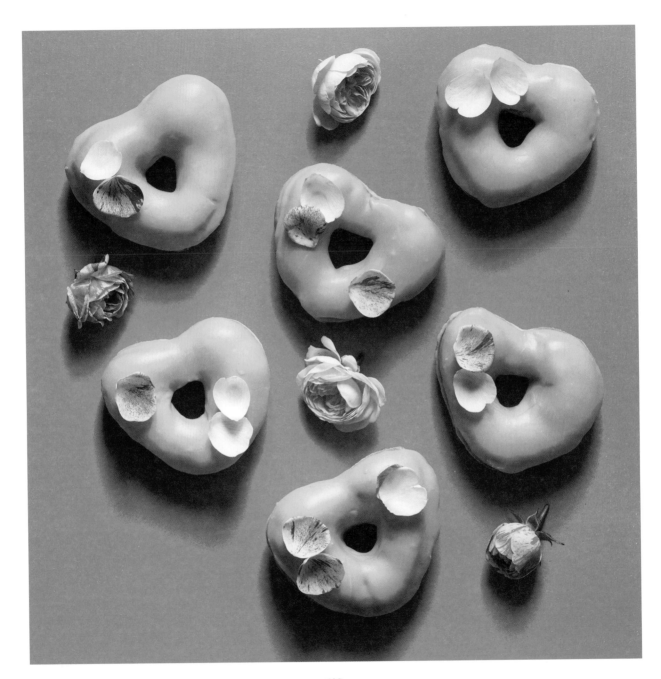

ROSE HEART VALENTINE'S DONUTS

If these pretty little hearts don't win bae over for Valentine's Day, nothing will.

Makes 12 regular donuts

1 batch of The Original dough → P.19

rose icing (frosting)

500 g (1 lb 2 oz/4 cups) icing
   (confectioner's) sugar
½ tsp rose water
50 ml (2 fl oz/3 tbsp) water
pink natural food colouring
edible rose petals

- - -

large and small heart-shaped cutters

→ We source our edible flowers online
from maddocksfarmorganics.co.uk

1   Cut out the donuts, using a large heart-shaped cutter. Cut out the centre of the donuts using a mini heart-shaped cutter. Bake or fry the donuts, following the instructions on page 21. Leave to cool on a wire rack.

2   To make the rose icing, place the icing sugar, rose water and half of the water in a bowl and stir. Gradually add the rest of the water, stirring continuously, until you end up with a smooth mixture. Add the food colouring and mix well.

3   Dunk each donut into the icing, covering the surface evenly. Gently pull the donut back up, keeping the top down and slowly spinning the donut by around 180 degrees or so, to let any excess drip back down into the bowl.

4   Top each donut with a rose petal and give to someone you love!

▲ CELEBRATE!

GIANT VANILLA DONUT CAKE

There's something sweetly nostalgic about vanilla birthday cake – though this guy has a little more flavour than the shop-bought fondant versions I remember as a kid and is super fun to make. Also, who doesn't want a giant donut for their birthday, amirite?

Makes 1 × 23 cm (9 in) cake

230 g (8 oz/2 sticks) unsalted butter, plus extra for greasing
230 g (8 oz/1 cup) caster (superfine) sugar
4 medium eggs
230 g (8 oz/1¾ cups) sifted self-raising flour
1 tsp baking powder
pinch of salt
2 tbsp full-fat (whole) milk (if needed)
1 batch of Vanilla Bean icing → P.25
pink natural food colouring

giant sprinkles

100 g (3½ oz) fondant icing (shop bought is fine)
natural food colouring in pastel blue, yellow, pink and lilac

---

23 cm (9 in) savarin ring tin (mould)

1 Preheat the oven to 180°C (350°F/Gas 4) and liberally grease the savarin tin (mould) with butter.
2 Put the butter and sugar in a mixing bowl and whisk until pale and fluffy.
3 Beat in the eggs, one at a time, adding a spoonful of flour with each egg. Gently fold in the rest of the flour, baking powder and salt, trying not to overwork it. Add the milk if it seems stiff.
4 Place the mixture into the cake tin and bake in the oven for 25–30 minutes, or until skewer or cocktail stick inserted in the centre should comes out clean. Leave to cool before transferring to a wire rack.
5 Place the vanilla bean icing into a bowl and add a drop of pink food colouring. Mix together and set aside.
6 To make the giant sprinkles, divide the fondant into 4 even pieces and colour each one with each of the shades of food colouring.

7 Using the palms of your hands, make small sausage shapes of around 1¼ cm (½ in) width with each of the colours. With a sharp knife, cut 3 cm (1¼ in) lengths from each sausage shape to make giant sprinkles.
8 Turn the cooled cake out onto a stand or dish. Give the icing a quick stir then pour it over the cake. Be quick and confident with it – you don't want it to begin to set before you've finished covering the cake, otherwise lumps will form. If the icing seems too thick, warm it up a little either in the microwave for a few seconds or in a pan on a low heat.
9 While the icing is still damp, press the fondant sprinkles onto the cake in a random formation.
10 Let the icing set before slicing up to serve!

PIÑATA DONUTS

When you bite into these guys you'll get an explosion of hidden Smarties! My fave kind of piñata.

**Makes 12 regular donuts
or 24 minis**

1 batch of The Original dough,
   fried or baked ⟶ P.19 & 21
   centres left in place during
   proving and cooking ⟶ note on P.47
200 g (7 oz/generous 1 cup) caster
   (superfine) sugar
175 g (6 oz/scant 1 cup) Mini Smarties®,
   or M&M Minis®
60 g (2 oz/⅓ cup) rainbow sprinkles, to decorate

white chocolate buttercream
175 g (6 oz/1½ sticks) unsalted butter
175 g (6 oz/1½ cups) icing (confectioner's) sugar
125 g (4 oz/generous ¾ cup) good-quality
   white chocolate, broken into pieces
   (or use white chocolate chips)
2 tbsp double (heavy) cream

---

10 cm (4 in) ring cutter
   or 6 cm (2½ in) mini ring cutter
piping bag

1 Using a sharp knife, carefully remove the centre of each donut, making sure you leave a little dough at the bottom to hold in the filling.
2 Place the donuts in a bowl with the sugar and toss to coat. You might need to do this one by one.
2 Fill the centre of each donut with Mini Smarties®, all the way to the top
3 For the buttercream, using either a stand mixer or electric whisk, whisk the butter until pale and fluffy (around 2 minutes). Add the icing sugar, one spoonful at time, mixing again in between each addition.
4 Melt the white chocolate either in the microwave for around 1 minute or in a glass bowl over a pan filled with 5 cm (2 in) water, on a low heat. Slowly pour the melted chocolate into the buttercream mixture, beating all the while.

5 Fold in the cream to soften it a little and transfer to a piping bag, cutting an opening measuring around 2.5 cm (1 in) in the tip of the bag. Twist the top of the bag to stop the buttercream escaping.
6 Pipe a dollop of the buttercream to each of the donuts and top with sprinkles.

◄ CELEBRATE!

PROSECCO & ORANGE DONUT TOWER

If you're into celebration cakes, this donut tower is the one for you. It's boozy, it's glittery and you can even have a game of donut Jenga with your mates when grabbing one.

Covers 24 minis

1 batch of The Original dough,
    fried or baked ⟶ P.19 & P.21
500 g (1 lb 2 oz/4 cups) icing (confectioner's)
    sugar
zest and juice of 2 oranges
3 tbsp Prosecco
gold edible glitter spray, to decorate

---

6 cm (2½ in) mini ring cutter

Note: If you don't want to waste a standard 750 ml (25 fl oz) bottle of Prosecco here, you can get smaller 250 ml (8½ fl oz) versions from most supermarkets. Stick a straw in the bottle once you're done and finish it off when the baking's over – the dream! For the glitter, the stuff in the push-pump bottles is my fave version.

1   Place the icing sugar and orange zest in a bowl and gradually add the orange juice, while stirring.
2   Mix in the Prosecco, one spoonful at a time, and stir until smooth.
3   Dip the donuts into the glaze, submerging each one to around halfway down and leave to set.
4   Once the icing has dried, spray the surface of the donuts with the edible glitter.

◄ CELEBRATE!

LETTER DONUTS

Birthday wishes, 'Marry me?'s, even dirty cuss words – we've made them all into donuts. Now it's your turn to have a go!

Makes 20 letters

1 batch of The Original dough ⟶ P.19
1 batch of The Homer icing ⟶ P.29
  or any icing of your choice!
a handful of rainbow sprinkles, to decorate

---

alphabet cutters

1   Cut out the donuts, using whichever letter cutters you'd like to make a message. Bake or fry, following the instructions on page 21, and leave to cool. Some donuts will take longer to cook than others, depending on the letters you choose.

2   Dunk each donut into the icing, covering the surface evenly. Gently pull the donut back up, keeping the top down and slowly spinning the donut by around 180 degrees or so, to let any excess drip back down into the bowl.

3   Scatter sprinkles over the top and serve to someone special.

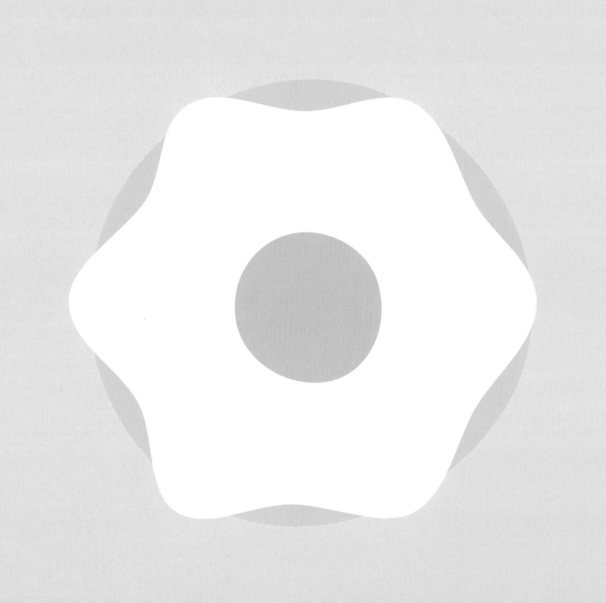

BRUNCH
CLUB

EGGS BENEDICT

Ham and eggs in a donut? Yes, please! Best brunch ever.

Makes 6 regular donuts

1 batch of The Original dough → P.19
1 tsp vinegar
pinch of salt
6 medium eggs
6 slices of good-quality ham

1   Make the dough as in the original recipe on page 19, up to step 8. Roll out the dough so it's super thin – around 3 mm (⅛ in) thick.
2   With a knife, cut the dough into 6 squares, each measuring around 15 cm (6 in). Set to one side, while you prep the rest.
3   Add the vinegar and salt to a pan of water and bring to the boil.
4   Once simmering, turn down the heat and break in an egg. Leave to simmer for 2 minutes exactly. Drain the egg on a piece of kitchen paper (towel) to soak up any excess water and leave to cool. Repeat until all 6 eggs are poached and cooled.

5   Fold the pieces of ham so they measure around 7 cm (2¾ in) and place one on top of each square of dough, at the centre. Top each piece of ham with a poached egg.
6   Make a parcel with the dough to cover the ham and eggs by folding in each corner of the square. Secure by pinching the dough tight, making sure there are no holes.
7   Leave to rise for around 30 minutes. If baking, spray your donuts with oil and bake for 10–15 minutes in a preheated oven at 220°C (430°F/Gas 7). Alternatively, fry them at 180°C (350°F) for 2 minutes and 30 seconds on each side, until golden brown.

BACON & MAPLE

Officially the best breakfast to cure a hangover with, ever! Skip the bacon sandwich and go straight in with this guy. All the sugary, meaty goodness you need.

Makes 12 regular donuts or 24 minis

1 batch of The Original,
  fried or baked → P.19 & P.21
400 g (14 oz/1¼ cups) icing
  (confectioner's) sugar
240 ml (8 fl oz/1 cup) maple syrup
300 g (10½ oz) dry cured smoked streaky bacon
---
10 cm (4 in) ring cutter

1 Chop the bacon into small pieces and put in a frying pan over a medium heat, stirring continually until crispy. Take off the heat and leave to cool.
2 Mix the icing sugar with the maple syrup until smooth.
3 Dip a donut, top down, into the bowl of icing to around halfway, and gently pull back up.
4 While the icing is still wet, sprinkle the bacon pieces so that they stick to the donuts.
5 Serve while still warm!

FIG & GOAT'S CHEESE

Super nice as an hors d'oeuvre in one hand with a glass of Prosecco in the other – the perfect party snack, donut style.

Makes 12 regular donuts or 24 minis

1 batch of The Original dough, fried or baked → P.19 & P.21 centres left in place during proving and cooking → note on P.47

fig conserve

800 g (1 lb 12 oz) ripe figs, plus more for decoration
800 g (1 lb 12 oz/3⅔ cups) caster (superfine) sugar
pinch salt
1 tbsp water
zest and juice of 2 lemons

goat's cream cheese

450 g (1 lb) soft goat's cheese
280 g (10 oz/1¼ cup) cream cheese
5 tbsp icing (confectioner's) sugar
200 ml (7 fl oz/generous ¾ cup) double (heavy) cream

---

10 cm (4 in) ring cutter
piping bag

1 Using a sharp knife, carefully remove the centre of each donut, making sure you leave a little dough at the bottom to hold in the filling.

2 To make the conserve, roughly chop the figs and place in a heavy-based saucepan with the sugar, salt, water and lemon zest and juice on a low heat.

3 Bring to the boil and simmer for around 20 minutes until the mixture has thickened. Set aside to cool.

4 To make the filling beat the goat's cheese, cream cheese and icing sugar together until smooth. Gradually add the double cream, continuing to beat until all lumps have disappeared and the mixture is smooth and creamy.

5 Using a spoon, spread 1 tablespoon of the fig conserve on to the top of each donut, spreading it around the surface to cover it evenly.

6 Place the goat's cheese mixture into a piping bag and cut a hole of around 2 cm (¾ in) at the tip. Pipe the mixture into the centre of each donut.

7 Quarter the remaining figs and place on top of the goat's cheese.

8 Serve straight away!

FAUX-NUTS

VEGAN DONUTS

These guys are super light and fluffy and taste really similar to our original dough recipe. In fact, a lot of people can't even tell the difference.

Makes 12 regular donuts or 24 minis

750 g (1½ lbs/5⅓ cups) strong white bread flour, plus extra for dusting

80 g (2½ oz/¾ cup) caster (superfine) sugar

60 g (2¾ oz/¼ cup) dairy-free margarine

15 g (¾ oz/2½ tsp) salt

21 g (⅔ oz/4½ tsp) instant dried yeast

egg substitute (such as aquafaba), (equivalent to 3 eggs), lightly whipped until foamy

290 ml (10 fl oz/1 cup) oat milk

120 ml (4 fl oz/½ cup) warm water

2 tbsp vegetable oil

1   Place the flour, sugar and margarine in a large bowl. Make 2 wells in the flour at opposite sides of the bowl and add the salt to one, and the yeast to the other.

2   Add the aquafaba and the oat milk.

3   If you're using a stand mixer, attach the dough hook and mix on the slowest speed setting, whilst slowly pouring the water into the dough mixture. If you don't have a stand mixer, use one hand to bring the dough together and the other to add the water. Once all the water has been added and all the ingredients have been incorporated, you'll have a sticky, wet mixture.

4   Knead in the mixer on a slow setting for 8 minutes or on a floured surface, using your hands, for 10 minutes. When it's been kneaded enough, it'll be smooth, elastic and have a shiny surface.

5   Put in a clean bowl and cover with a damp tea towel until doubled in size (this can take anything between 30–90 minutes, depending on the temperature of your kitchen).

6   Grease 2 baking trays with 1 tablespoon of vegetable oil each.

7   Cover your hands with flour and sprinkle some over your work surface. Tip out the dough and knead with your hands a little to form a ball.

8   Sprinkle the rolling pin with flour and roll out the dough to around 2 cm (¾ in) thick.

9   Use a cutter to cut out shapes and place on the greased trays, spacing them out. Knead any leftover dough and roll out to repeat the process. Leave to rise for around 10–20 minutes, until the dough springs back when you touch it. Cook the dough using one of the methods on page 21.

VEGAN-FRIENDLY
ICINGS & FILLINGS

Vegan icing (frosting) & filling recipes:

- Vanilla Bean, substituting the milk for oat or almond milk (P.25)
- The Homer (P.29)
- Blood Orange (P.33)
- Matcha substituting the milk for oat or almond milk (P.35)
- Hibiscus (P.37)
- Coffee & Walnut (P.39)
- Apple Pie, with almond or oat milk in the vanilla glaze (P.53)
- Prosecco & Orange (P.115)

Or try:

- Mixing the Vanilla Bean icing (page 25, made with dairy-free milk) with crushed Oreos
- Using Lotus Biscoff® caramel spread as a filling, topped with Biscoff crumbs and melted dairy-free dark chocolate, such as Green & Black's®
- Making the Jay Dee recipe (page 27) using coconut milk instead of double (heavy) cream for a dreamy chocolate glaze.

GLUTEN-FREE
VANILLA DONUTS

These beauties are made using a cake mixture and then baked in a donut tin (pan).

Makes 12 ring donuts or 24 minis

180 g (6½ oz/1¾ sticks) unsalted butter, plus extra for greasing tin
180 g (6½ oz/¾ cup) caster (superfine) sugar
1 tsp vanilla bean paste
3 medium eggs
180 g (6½ oz/1¾ cups) sifted gluten-free self-raising flour (use one containing xanthan gum)
1 tsp gluten-free baking powder
2 tbsp full-fat (whole) milk (if needed)
pinch of salt

vanilla bean icing (frosting)
500 g (1 lb 2 oz/4 cups) icing (confectioner's) sugar
½ tsp vanilla bean paste
30 ml (2 fl oz/2 tbsp) full-fat (whole) milk
---
2 × 12-hole donut tin (pan)
or 2 × 6-hole donut tin (pan)

1   Preheat the oven to 180°C (350°F fan/Gas 4) and liberally grease the donut tin (pan) with butter.
2   Put the butter, sugar and vanilla bean paste in a mixing bowl and whisk until super pale and fluffy.
3   Beat in the eggs, one at a time, each with a spoonful of flour.
4   Gently fold in the rest of the flour with the baking powder and salt and add the milk if the mixture seems stiff.
5   Put around 1 tablespoon of mixture into each donut ring and spread evenly.
6   Bake in the oven for 10–15 minutes, until a skewer

or cocktail stick inserted into the centre comes out clean. Leave to cool before transferring to a wire rack.
7   To make the icing, place the icing sugar, vanilla bean paste and half of the milk into a bowl and stir.
8   Gradually add the rest of the milk, stirring, until you end up with a smooth mixture.
9   Carefully dunk each donut into the bowl until the icing covers it around halfway.
10   Gently pull the donut back up, keeping the top down and slowly spinning the donut around by 180 degrees or so, to let any excess drip back down into the bowl.

GLUTEN-FREE
CHOCOLATE DONUTS

Chocolate cake donuts with a chocolate glaze – not a hint of gluten in sight.

Makes 12 regular donuts

a small knob of unsalted butter, for greasing

200 g (7 oz/1 ⅓ cups) self-raising gluten-free flour (use one containing xanthan gum)

75 g (2½ oz/⅔ cup) cocoa powder

pinch of salt

200 g (7 oz/scant 1 cup) caster (superfine) sugar

½ tsp bicarbonate soda

180 ml (6½ fl oz/⅔ cup) sour cream

1 tsp vanilla bean paste

125 ml (4 fl oz/½ cup) vegetable oil

2 medium eggs

125 ml (4 fl oz/½ cup) warm water

dark chocolate ganache

300 ml (10 fl oz/1¼ cups) double (heavy) cream

150 g (5 oz/1 cup) dark chocolate chips (at least 70% cocoa solids)

30 g (1 oz/¼ cup) cacao nibs

rainbow-colour sprinkles, for decoration

---

2 × 6-hole donut tin (pan)

1   Preheat the oven to 180°C (350°F fan/Gas 4) and liberally grease the donut tin (pan) with butter.

2   Mix together the dry ingredients in a bowl, make a well and add the sour cream, vanilla bean paste, vegetable oil, eggs and water, mixing after each addition.

3   Put around 1 tablespoon of mixture into each donut ring and spread evenly.

4   Bake in the oven for 15 minutes, until a skewer or cocktail stick inserted into the centre comes out clean, and leave to cool before transferring to a cooling rack.

5   To make the ganache, heat the double cream over a medium heat until bubble start to form on the surface. Put the chocolate chips in a medium-sized heatproof bowl and pour over hot cream.

6   Using a spatula, give the mixture a good stir, picking up any lumps of chocolate left at the bottom. Leave it for 2 minutes and then give it another stir until the chocolate has melted.

7   Carefully dunk each donut into the bowl until the icing covers it around halfway.

8   Gently pull the donut back up, keeping the top down and slowly spinning the donut by around 180 degrees or so, to let any excess drip back down into the bowl.

9   Scatter with the sprinkles and devour.

◂ FAUX-NUTS

GLUTEN-FREE & VEGAN
LEMON DONUTS

I used to think that dairy-free, gluten-free and egg-free meant taste-free, but thanks to some great new gluten-free flours and soya yoghurts, you can make some super tasty bakes. These guys are super squidgy and lemony.

Makes 12 regular donuts

125 g (4 oz/½ cup) dairy-free margarine, plus extra for greasing

190 g (6½ oz/scant 1 cup) caster (superfine) sugar

3 lemons

125 g (4 oz/1¼ cups) ground almonds (almond meal)

90 g (3¼ oz/generous ½ cup) gluten-free plain (all-purpose) flour (use one containing xanthan gum)

75 g (2½ oz/⅓ cup) polenta

1½ tsp bicarbonate of soda (baking soda)

1 tsp baking powder

250 ml (8½ fl oz/1 cup) soya yoghurt

1½ tbsp cornflour (cornstarch)

30 g (1 oz/2 tbsp) granulated sugar

60 g (2 oz/¼ cup) caster (superfine) sugar

lemon glaze

400 g (14 oz/¾ cup) icing (confectioner's) sugar

4 tbsp lemon juice (use the juice from one of the lemons, above)

---

2 × 6-hole donut tin (pan)

1 Preheat oven to 180°C (350°F/Gas 4) and liberally grease the donut tin (pan) with margarine.

2 Cream together the margarine and sugar until light and fluffy. Zest 2 of the lemons and add to the mixture.

3 Stir in the almonds, flour, polenta, bicarbonate of soda, baking powder, yoghurt and lemon zest to the creamed margarine, and whisk.

4 Juice one of the lemons and mix together with the cornflour in a bowl. Juice another lemon and heat in a saucepan with the granulated sugar, before adding the lemon juice and cornflour mix, whisking continuously. Add to the cake mixture.

5 Put around 1 tablespoon of mixture into each donut ring and spread evenly.

6 Bake in the oven for 10–15 minutes, or until just beginning to turn golden. Leave to cool before transferring out onto a wire rack.

7 Zest the remaining lemon and mix in a bowl with the caster sugar to make candied peel. Leave to one side.

8 To make the lemon glaze, juice the lemon you've just zested and add 4 tablespoons of the lemon juice to the icing sugar. Mix well. Spoon the glaze over the donuts and sprinkle over the candied lemon peel.

JAMS, CUSTARDS & SAUCES

From left to right: Italian Meringue (page 143); Raspberry Coulis, (page 146); Lemon Curd (page 142); Crème Pâtissière (page 140); Salted Caramel (page 141); Pineapple Jam (page 145); Blueberry Compote (page 144)

CRÈME PÂTISSIÈRE

This seems very cheffy but crème pâtissière is one of those recipes that's always much easier to make than you think. Just make sure to follow all of the steps exactly as it can turn into scrambled eggs if you're too hasty.

Makes approx. 600 g (1lb 7 oz)

8 medium egg yolks
140 g (5 oz/⅔ cup) caster (superfine) sugar
35 g (1 oz/2 tbsp) plain (all-purpose) flour
35 g (1 oz/2 tbsp) cornflour (cornstarch)
700 ml (23½ fl oz/3 cups) full-fat (whole) milk
1 tsp vanilla bean paste
1 tbsp icing (confectioner's) sugar

1   Whisk the egg yolks and sugar in a bowl until pale and fluffy – around 2 minutes in a stand mixer and 5 minutes by hand.

2   Add the flour and cornflour and whisk again until combined.

3   Put the milk and vanilla bean paste in a large saucepan and heat until it reaches a simmer, stirring constantly.

4   Remove from the heat and leave to cool for 2 minutes.

5   Whisking all the time, slowly pour half of the warm milk onto the egg yolk mixture, then transfer the mixture to the pan with the remaining milk.

6   Put the pan back onto the heat and bring to the boil, whisking continuously. After a couple of minutes, it will become thick and smooth.

7   Pour the mixture into either a clean bowl or plastic tub and dust with icing sugar. Leave at room temperature to cool down before transferring to the fridge where it will keep for up to 24 hours.

SALTED CARAMEL

I'll be honest, making caramel still kind of scares me! It's those seconds of hesitation just before the sugar turns brown that gets me in sweats. I'm always like: 'Is now the time to add the butter?! Is it too early?! Has it burnt? What am I doing?!' The key things to remember are: 1) Watch it like a hawk, 2) Be very careful when holding your hands near the pan and 3) Never ever, ever, ever touch it – cos you gon' get burrrnnnnt. And caramel burns are not fun. It's worth overcoming the fear though and once it's done, it keeps for 2 weeks in the fridge.

Makes approx. 400 ml (13 fl oz)

200 g (7 oz/scant 1 cup) caster (superfine) sugar
100 g (3½ oz/⅘ stick) unsalted butter
100ml (3½ fl oz/scant ½ cup) double (heavy) cream
1 tsp salt

1   Heat the sugar in a saucepan over a medium heat, watching it continually and swirling in the pan until it dissolves and turns to a medium amber colour.

2   As soon as it turns amber, add the butter and stir, being careful not to burn yourself with bubbles. Carry on stirring for a couple of minutes.

3   Slowly add the cream to the pan – it will splatter and release steam as you add it so watch out.

4   Simmer for 1 minute, add the salt and leave to cool. It will be ready to use in 2–3 hours and keeps for 2 weeks in the fridge.

LEMON CURD

My nana Doris came up with this recipe for gooey, lemony goodness and it is just the best. If you have leftovers, it's amazing with lemon polenta cake and also makes every slice of toast one hundred per cent better.

Makes approx. 400 ml (13 fl oz)

2 medium eggs
450 g (1 lb/2 cups) (superfine) sugar
50 g (1¾ oz/½ stick) unsalted butter
juice and zest of 2 lemons

1 In a large glass bowl, beat the eggs before adding the rest of the ingredients.
2 Place the bowl on top of a pan of boiling water, making sure that the bowl does not touch the water underneath.
3 Stir occasionally until the mixture begins to thicken, then cook for a further 15 minutes, stirring frequently.
4 Transfer into sterilised jars and keep for up to 6 months in the fridge.

ITALIAN MERINGUE

This stuff is addictive! It goes with everything and works especially well with citrus flavours. Be careful not to overmix the egg whites, otherwise you'll end up a with curdled mess. Also, if making it on a hot day, be sure to put it in the fridge until ready to use or it will separate.

Makes approx. 350 g (12 oz)

4 medium egg whites
225 g (8 oz/1 cup) caster (superfine) sugar
6 tbsp water

1 Beat the egg whites until they form stiff peaks. The mixture should hold its shape when the whisk is removed.

2 Make a sugar syrup by placing the sugar and water in a pan over a medium heat until the sugar has dissolved and the temperature reaches 120°C (248°F). If any grains of sugar stick on the side of the pan, brush them off with a pastry brush and dip back down into the syrup mixture. This will stop the mixture from becoming lumpy.

3 Once the syrup has reached 120°C (248°F), slowly pour it onto the egg whites, whisking them as you go.

4 Continue to whisk until all the syrup has been used and the egg whites have cooled.

5 Place into a clean bowl and refrigerate until needed for up to 2 days.

BLUEBERRY COMPOTE

I love the purple hue of this stuff, especially when rippled through my cheesecake mixture as on page 55. The lemon juice gives it a sharp edge and makes it even tastier.

Makes approx. 250 ml (8½ fl oz)

400 g (14 oz/2½ cups) blueberries
1 tbsp honey
juice of 1 lemon

1 Place all of the ingredients into a pan on a medium heat.
2 As it begins to simmer, turn down the heat and leave for 10–15 minutes until the blueberries are soft.
3 Transfer to a sterilised jar and keep in the fridge for up to 2 weeks.

PINEAPPLE JAM

You can, of course, use a shop-bought version of this if you don't fancy having a go. There is something quite therapeutic about cutting up a pineapple into tiny pieces and watching it turn to goo — or maybe I'm just weird.

Makes approx. 250 g (8½ oz)

1 pineapple
200 ml (7 fl oz/generous ¾ cup) water
400 g (14 oz/1¾ cups) jam sugar
juice of 2 lemons

1 Chop the pineapple and remove the skin.
2 Chop the flesh into chunks and put into a pan with the water on a medium heat for around 30 minutes until soft.
3 Add the jam sugar and lemon juice and simmer until thick, around 30–40 minutes.
4 Transfer into sterilised jars and store for up to 12 months.

RASPBERRY COULIS

The basis for The Homer (page 29) our famous pink icing. This raspberry coulis uses lemon juice to make it extra tangy and fruity.

Makes approx. 250 ml (8½ fl oz)

400 g (14 oz/3¼ cups) raspberries
8 tbsp icing (confectioner's) sugar
juice of 2 lemons

1 Put the raspberries, icing sugar and lemon juice into a pan and place on a low heat until the raspberries start to break down.
2 Take off the heat and either transfer to a food processer or pulse with a hand-blender and blitz until smooth.
3 Once smooth, pass through a sieve to remove any pips and place into a clean bowl or sterilised glass jar. Keeps in the fridge for up to 1 week.

MAKE YOUR OWN SPRINKLES

Making your own sprinkles is super easy to do! Plus, by making them yourself you can guarantee that no nasty stuff has gone into them. Feel free to go with your inner Picasso and choose your own colours – I've gone for some typical mixed ones here.

Makes approx. 250 g (8½ oz)

250 g (9 oz/2 cups) icing (confectioner's) sugar
1 medium egg white
natural food colouring in pink, yellow, blue
   and green

1   Mix the icing sugar with the egg white until combined – it should have a very gluey and thick consistency.

2   Divide the icing into 4 bowls and squeeze a little of each food colour in each one, mixing well.

3   Place the contents of each bowl into a separate piping bag and snip at the end to make a very small hole.

4   Place a sheet of baking paper onto a level surface and pipe lines in each colour of icing directly onto the sheet.

The icing will be very thick so you need a steady hand! Don't worry if there are gaps between the lines, you won't notice this later.

5   Leave to dry for at least 2 hours before cutting the sprinkles up into tiny strips using a sharp knife.

6   Roll the paper up into a cylinder and give it a tap against the surface to remove any sprinkles that have got stuck. Store in an airtight container. They should keep for up to 1 month.

VICKY'S DONUTS™

Vicky's Donuts™ has been featured in *Time Out*, *Evening Standard*, *InStyle*, *BuzzFeed*, *LOOK*, *ELLE*, *Betty Magazine*, *BRIDES* and *The Debrief* and counts brands like Facebook, BBC, L'Oréal, Soap & Glory, Puma, Topshop and ASOS amongst its huge customer base. Vicky takes her tasty donuts to festivals, events and exclusive parties, is a part of London street food collective, KERB, and has supplied to retailers such as Selfridges, London. She also hosts workshops in London to spread the donutty lovin'.

Follow Vicky on Instagram @**vickysdonuts** or visit **vickysdonuts.com**

THANK YOU!

I'd like to say a HUGE thanks to everyone at Hardie Grant for giving me the opportunity to write a book. It's a dream I've had for ages and you guys made it happen – THANK YOU! Especially to Kajal Mistry for having the vision to turn what I do into printed pages and for working her butt off to get it right. Also to Molly Ahuja for the painstaking edits and amends (sorry, Molly). To Marketing and Sales too for working hard to make this book a success.

Mama bear, my little pillar of strength. Thank you for teaching me from a young age that girls rule - not only has it enabled me to be a girl boss that takes no $hit but it's also placed a huge importance on surrounding myself with a circle of amazing women that inspire me everyday. Your belief in me has kept me going at the hardest of times and I am so grateful for your help in getting me to where I am now (and I don't just mean all the washing up I made you do).

Thanks to Joe Woodhouse for the beautiful photography (and the amazing home cooking) and to Studio Thomas for the awesome design skills. Jacqui Melville for your prop-sourcing expertise and to Ben Clark for being super supportive and (gently) nudging me when it came to deadline time.

Papa G, you taught me that anything can be achieved as long as you work your butt off and stay focused, and who woulda thought you were right?! I thought you might freak out when I first told you I wanted to make donuts instead of working in an office but you've been super supportive from the start. Love you lots big man.

Thank you to my amazing donut buddy and assistant Kim Lucas. You go above and beyond of whatever is asked and always encourage me to think big when all I want to do is sleep! You are truly incredible and I donut know what I'd do without you.

Ben Lifton – thank you for being my number donut one fan and to Demi, Nilly, Craig and Harriet for being the bestest friends I could ask for.

Nett and Steve, thank you for emigrating to Canada and introducing me to the world of donuts! Some of my fave childhood memories are of hanging out in your house, snow falling outside, wrapped up in PJs and eating chocolate glazed goodies for breakfast. You guys are the best.

Studio Moross for helping me out before I even started - you guys are awesome and the offer of free donuts 4 lyfe will always stand.

Team Brrr – SJ, Chris and Jon - thank you for the bazillion taste-tests I made you do! And super sorry for all those runs you had to go on afterwards.

To anyone that's ever bought a donut from our little bakery, attended a workshop of ours or followed us on Instagram - THANK YOU!

And finally to you for reading this and for buying this book – I hope it brings a whole lot of donut happiness into your life and teaches you lots of new skills that encourage you to get creative in the kitchen!

INDEX